Ozana Giusca

Business Unlimited
Smarter Profits Faster

- Volume 6 -

Sustain Your Business Long-Term

101 Zero-Cost Tactics to Take Your Company to the Next Level

Amaze Yourself With What YOU Can Achieve Further!

Copyright © 2017 Ozana Giusca
All rights reserved.

ISBN-13: 978-1978361898
ISBN-10: 1978361890

To all the business owners and entrepreneurs I have worked with: thank you for entrusting me with growing your business.

To my team, who have put so much effort into building Tooliers, the high-end business growth tools and programs that are transforming businesses around the world, a big thank you for going through the ups and downs with me.

Thank you for helping me with this book. We wouldn't be here without your dedication and contribution!

I would like to name the Tooliers core team: Vali, Dragos, Sorana & Catalina. You are like family to me! I am so grateful you joined me in my journey!

Table of Contents

Foreword	V
Preface	VII
My Story	IX
Introduction	1
Bonus • Steady Growth - Systematize Your Business	4
Tactic #1 • Follow a System	5
Tactics #2- #71 are in Volumes 1-5	
Sustain Your Business Long-Term	12
Tactic #72 • Determine Your Product's 'Buying Criteria'	13
Tactic #73 • Create Your X-Factor	17
Tactic #74 • Use 'Core Story'	22
Tactic #75 • Train Everyone in Your Company to Say Something Valuable about Your Company	26
Tactic #76 • Communicate Your Ultimate Strategic Position	30
Tactic #77 • Help Your Customers Achieve More Success	34
Tactic #78 • Create Clear Accountability within Your Company	38
Tactic #79 • Understand Your Business. Really!	42
Tactic #80 • Clarify Your Vision	47
Tactic #81 • Create an Unstoppable Pre-emptive Anti-Competition Strategy	50
Tactic #82 • Inspire High Levels of Brand Loyalty	54
Tactic #83 • Build Trust, Credibility and Respect	58
Tactic #84 • Focus on What People Buy, Not on Your Profits or Sales	62
Tactic #85 • Associate with Trusted Organizations	66
Tactic #86 • Be 'Online Social'	71
Smart Business System™	76
Bonus • Love Letter	88
Love Letter Template	90
Love Letter Example	91
Glossary of Terms	94

Foreword

The world is changing so fast. These events are opportunities for those who grab them, and at the same time can negatively affect those who do not take action. Most small businesses find it harder to break through their current level. They reach a plateau and do not know what step to take next, or go beyond 'small' and lose the plot.

There is so much information available now about how to run a successful business, but the challenge is to find meaning within this information and to use it appropriately to optimize and grow your business. In my experience as a small business consultant, I have seen a lot of business owners who cannot simply and quickly explain what they do, let alone generate interest and sell their products or services. I also see that entrepreneurs have dreams and goals, yet 80% of their time is spent on things that have no link whatsoever with their objectives. If they do not focus on what is needed to achieve their goals, how can they get there?

If you are looking for a very hands-on approach to building your business from the ground up, Ozana has nailed it in *Business Unlimited*. What a purposeful read for anyone who is an entrepreneur or small business owner. As you continue on your business or career journey, you will face real challenges that may deter you from achieving your biggest goals. The tactics in this book will keep you on track and help you reach your goals in record time.

In our lives we have the opportunity to do it the hard way or to learn from what the experts do, and then do it better. Ozana has been trained by some of the best in the business, including business and marketing guru Jay Abraham. In this new book you will discover key observations and ingredients to create even more success in your life and business. The real-world examples, as well as the practical exercises at the end of each tactic, also ensure this is a user-friendly manual to reaching business success.

Foreword

In *Business Unlimited*, you will learn to see the bigger picture of your business as well as discover the importance of *systematically* improving it; that is, by prioritizing and focusing on those areas that most need improvement. You will learn to identify your best customers; let go of any customers who do not lift your business; learn from your competitors; and fulfil the core purpose of every business: providing *real value* to your customers. You will also discover how creating the right kind of partnerships will grow your business with little extra effort on your part. Business owners will find the tactics on closing sales and creating urgency especially valuable. You will also see how essential it is to build relationships both with your best customers and your team.

This book is also brutally honest about areas in which business owners tend to waste time and resources – and provides a wealth of best practices for time management; this includes a reminder to employ the time-saving advantages of certain technologies. You will also be encouraged to reflect and act upon your role as a leader and to go beyond merely managing your business to making sure it leads to the kind of life and lifestyle you desire. Aspects like personal branding, networking and being open to change are also discussed. Finally, you will clarify your vision in order to take your brand into the future and be left with a business that is dynamic and that constantly strives for – and achieves – improvement and growth.

The bottom line: if you are ready to increase your success rate today, take the time to read this mind-expanding book two to three times, and then implement the ideas that are shared here.

Bill Walsh

America's Small Business Expert

Website: billwalsh360.com

Preface

If you answer YES! to any of these statements, this book is for you.

- You have achieved some success with your business, but seem unable to grow it further.
- You are not satisfied with where your business is.
- You are not getting enough from your business (you are not getting enough recognition or enough money, or you have not succeeded in fully achieving your Objectives).
- Work is taking over your life and you have no time for family, relaxation, or travel.
- You are still struggling to make a living.
- You are bored with your work! You want something more challenging and fun.
- You are missing something, but you're not sure exactly what.
- There are some areas you do not understand (for example, finance) or you are passionate about your product, but you cannot sell it.
- You just want to be sure that you are on top of things and that your business is on the right track.
- You have some ideas for new businesses, but are not quite sure how to go about it.
- You want new challenges, but you need your current business to continue to run for various reasons (financial, community).
- Your turnover and/or profits have started decreasing.
- You can anticipate a disaster but you cannot tell what exactly is happening.
- Your best employees have started to leave.
- You have lost your biggest client.
- You seem to deliver good quality but your clients are still not prepared to pay what you'd like for your products.
- There has been a recent change in your company's industry or outside

environment and this has had a great impact on your business.
- You and your staff are working too hard and it is just not fair on any of you (especially given the results you achieve).
- You consider your company a victim of your crisis, a system, or something else.
- Your business has stopped serving the community.
- Your business is growing quickly and you are struggling to manage it. It is becoming too complex for you to run on your own.
- Your life is too stressful. There are just too many problems that need to be solved by you, the business owner.
- You and your co-owners have trouble running the business together.
- Your business has started experiencing problems or you foresee problems, but you don't know what to do about them.
- You have accumulated too much debt in your company and can no longer sustain it.
- You simply want to discover the latest strategies that Fortune 500 companies use for their success!

My Story

I want to take a few minutes to ask you the questions that are on every small business owner's mind:

- What is the REAL secret behind businesses that generate more profits while their owners are enjoying life and doing what they want, when they want?
- Can I get more customers to call us instead of *us* chasing *them*?
- How can I get a great team of committed employees to work hard so we grow the business together?
- Is there any way to feel happier with my business and really achieve what I set my mind to?
- Ultimately, how can I, a small business owner, entrepreneur or freelance expert, make a difference in the world?

I get asked these questions all the time and it's why I wrote this book. Via this book, the tools, programs, events we deliver, I provide the answers to these questions, and many more.

Before you dig in, let me tell you a little about myself...

In 2007 my life seemed perfect. I was a rising star, doing everything most people would love to do.

After attaining my MBA from Cass Business School, London in 2000, I worked in the City for a few years. In 2003, I set up my own consulting firm, where I advised on selling a few companies and raised hundreds of millions in bank finance for various projects.

While my business generated a decent income, I knew I was on my way to support other entrepreneurs help more people and make a bigger impact.

With a team of 12 consultants, I was living my dream. I could party, travel, wear my favorite brands...

My Story

I bought a flat, then another one, then an office for our company, a new car… until the financial crisis hit my business badly, as happened with thousands of businesses around the world.

All of a sudden money stopped flowing in. The banks withdrew from financing our transactions; those hundreds of thousands of dollars in success fees never arrived; and ongoing consulting projects got put on hold. No more new business meant no more cash.

Imagine: By January 2009, I had let most of my team go. For me, they were not just staff, they were *family*. And they were damn good at what they did.

With more than a million dollars in debt, I could no longer pay the bank. Many sleepless nights followed… I felt ashamed, convinced people would point a finger at me, accuse me of not paying my debts. I got scared thinking about a potential bad credit rating and that I might never be able to get a loan again.

I felt my reputation as an honest, trustworthy businessperson was ruined as I couldn't pay my debts.

I had no money coming in and was borrowing on a monthly basis to pay my two remaining staff members. I was driving to my father every weekend to get food for the week for me and my partner.

It seemed that every phone call I got, every email I received, brought more bad news.

Watch this: my phone service provider threatening to end my contract should I not pay my bills. Imagine trying to save a business without a phone connection or access to the internet!

That was it, I decided. *Enough!* I borrowed more money and paid for an event in London where 15 successful entrepreneurs shared their strategies on how they became profitable. I learned about online marketing, selling one-to-many via events and social media advertising. Most importantly I realized the need to be visible to the right audience.

My Story

How many of these tactics do you think I applied? None! Because I soon realized I was in the wrong business anyway. Yep, this was my biggest take-away from the conference. I realized there was nothing special about me or my business, nothing that would get clients to choose our services.

There were too many people doing the same thing, making it difficult to differentiate myself.

As I had all this cutting edge knowledge, I started applying it to the businesses of former clients, and friends. And *this* is how I started earning again…

It turned out my consulting business was not the only business lacking proper business knowledge! In fact, most small businesses lack such knowledge – they are usually set up based on an opportunity the founder sees, based on the founder's skills and abilities. Yet businesses are complex and no entrepreneur can know it all; certainly no one can handle everything.

I also discovered my special gift: being able to identify where a business is leaving money on the table and how they can double or even triple their profits by making a few important changes.

My skill became immediately obvious as I managed to achieve:

- **30% increase in Sales within a month** for a client in hospitality (hotel) and a **287% increase in their online bookings within three months.** Their occupancy rate was 10% when we started working together – now it's in excess of 50%.

- **8 Sales during the first workshop** for a weight loss solution – a full house event achieved within five days of promotion. In fact, we had to close the doors and leave people outside disappointed.

- **$40,000 in Sales generated for a book** that had been sitting idle on Amazon before

> *With the right tools YOU too can turn your business around*

My Story

we started working with the author/chiropractor.

- **15% increase in Sales** for the main distributor of promotional materials, who already had 50% market share.

Over the past three years, I have personally helped more than 100 companies achieve massive growth. Some companies increased Sales by 30% within the first month of working with us; others tripled their Sales within a year.

I put all the knowledge I gathered – and much more – into what is today known as **Business Lens™**, a toolkit to identify what business owners don't do well or enough of in their company. This is **a tool that reveals the naked truth about any business**. It measures, mathematically, the gap between your company and Best Practices. The bigger the gap, the more growth potential the company has. Plus, it shows business owners where they need to focus to maximize Sales and profits.

This was the start of Tooliers, the platform with Smart Business solutions for small enterprises to increase profitability and become leaders in their niche. We now have clients around the globe and what's most important is not that we are making money, but that we help those who need us and our tools to smarten their businesses and achieve bigger profits faster.

Above all, I am proud of having built something that lasts beyond me. I know people will benefit from my current activities even after I am no longer here.

What's really in it for me? Or you?

> *When you focus on the right things in your business, you have the recipe to success*

FREEDOM!

The freedom to do what I want, when I want; to live anywhere in the world... and most importantly to be ME!

> *So what does this have to do with you and your business?*

You too can have the FREEDOM you want!

And I guess this is one reason you are reading this – you know you can do more and you want to.

The economy changes rapidly these days. As a small business owner, it is easy to run your business as if lost in a dark forest, thinking only of *survival*. You might forget about the destination. You are most likely involved with paying the next bill, dealing with a crisis after your best employee has left, trying to make up for that lost customer, deciding what kind of paper to buy for the copy machine and many other activities that keep you 'busy' and working hard.

But do you work *smart*? What if there was **a better way to achieve those dreams** you had when you started your business?

One third of business owners **want to grow their businesses, but don't know how and where to start**. The rest would like to maintain their business. The reality, however, is that 80% of businesses fail in the first five years and 96% in the first 10 years (this according to Michael Gerber, author of The *E-Myth*).

These facts also inspired me to write this book. I want to help YOU, a business owner, to *enjoy* your entrepreneurship. I want to help driven entrepreneurs just like you to achieve the success you deserve.

Business Unlimited is a collection of Best Practices I have seen and learned during my 20-year career in professional services. I learned about these tactics from seminars, workshops, conferences and summits, and I have tried and tested them on my business and on our clients' businesses. When you master the tactics that follow, you will be able to compete with multinational companies, with Fortune 500 companies, as their equal. Because you know what? They use exactly the same tactics you are about to discover.

This book is part of my mission to empower 1,000,000 entrepreneurs to change the world while they achieve their personal and professional objectives fast, with ease.

Happy reading and enjoy the transformation of your business!

Ozana

Your Smarter Profits Accelerator

P.S. If you are serious about growing your Sales and profits, raising your profile and helping way more people, I invite you to join any of my online or live Master Classes and bootcamps.

Visit My Events Page *(www.ozanagiusca.com/my-events)* to get the updated schedule of my events and register to those most suitable for you.

Why have I written this book?

I wrote this book because I believe YOU can achieve much more especially in today's economy, which is the best possible environment for driven entrepreneurs and small businesses to really take off and finally get to the next level, especially because of the Internet and technology developments.

I believe that small businesses are changing the world and making it a better place... provided they deploy the right systems. Thus, this book is about a systematic approach to business so you achieve your dreams and gain the respect you deserve.

Turning around my own company from the brink of bankruptcy in 2008 to a business selling on all continents was an incredible journey. Having been through 3 years with no sales (before Tooliers took off), I made every possible mistake. I also realised that business can be fun. So I made it my mission to empower 1,000,000 entrepreneurs to make a bigger impact, by proving them with full clarity on their business, and, of course, the right tools. Bottom line, I want to reduce the entrepreneurial struggle by encouraging small business owners and experts to first think strategically and then implement any tactic they consider. This way, they finally get results quickly with no stress or overwhelm.

This book is about sharing some of the lessons we've learnt so you build a profitable business and unleash your unlimited potential... **hence BUSINESS UNLIMITED**.

You hear me talk about Smart Business, which is the vehicle to get there... A Smart Business is flexible in approach, leverages what you have and know, and systematically attracts clients online so you scale and grow exponentially. This, of course, enables you, its founder and commander, to be anywhere you want, and not chained to your desk 16 hours per day.

My Story

Regardless of being early stage or a successful entrepreneur, if you are driven to achieve more, to create more value, to serve more people and improve their lives while you get what you want, then I would love to support you in your journey.

Let's change the world together!

Introduction

How to use this book

You don't have to start with Tactic 1, or to read this collection chronologically. Start with the tactic that feels the most interesting to you. Each tactic addresses a different Stage of a business. You may find one tactic more relevant than another. Read the relevant ones first and feel free to jump from one tactic to another.

You will see that each of the 101 Tactics concludes with a short exercise that will make it easy to apply the tactic to your business. If you are serious about growing your business, it is essential that you *decide how to apply* the tactic you have just read and *do the exercises* that follow. While doing the exercises, write down whatever comes to mind.

Don't get overwhelmed by all the information in this book. You don't have to use it all at once. However, you will be surprised by how much of this book applies to you and your business. Take the knowledge on board, and don't get desperate if you can't find a way of using it on the spot. The more you practice using these tactics, the more ideas you will get – in time you may even find ways to use those tactics you thought were not relevant to your business.

Revisit the book as your business Needs and Goals change. Reread certain tactics, or tackle new ones. This book may well become your 'Bible for a Smarter Business'.

Introduction

The finer details

Definitions of all words or terms that appear in **bold and italics** or starting with Caps can be found in the Glossary of Terms.

I use **customer** as a generic term. In your industry, you may prefer the word client, visitor, guest, user, or patient, for example.

I use examples from **a range of industries**. Feel free to adapt and apply the tactics to your own business.

Throughout the book, I use **products** and **services** interchangeably. Note, however, that an **offering** is not the same as a product or service. For our purposes, an offering refers to the product or service combined with its price, packaging and positioning. So, product X as offering A is sold for $100 as a stand-alone product. Product X could also be packaged as offering B, which includes another item or addresses a different market or just has a different packaging, and sells for $200.

Example:

> Cashew nuts can be sold in large quantities (tons) to wholesalers, who then repackage the nuts in smaller quantities (say 1 kilogram) to be sold at the market. Those same cashew nuts can be sold in supermarkets in packs of 300 grams; these look more attractive and command a higher price. Or the cashew nuts can be sold per 100 grams in a high-end bar, for a premium price.
>
> The product is the same – cashew nuts – but with different packaging and/or positioning, it becomes a different offering and commands a different price.
>
> The target market could be the same or different. I could be buying a 1 kg pack at the market, but I could also buy the 300 gram packs in gas stations.

Introducing Tooliers®

Tooliers® (www.tooliers.com) is THE latform with high-end business growth solutions to empower entrepreneurs to build their SMART business so they increase profitability, reduce struggle and become leaders in their niche.

Business Lens™ is the digital mirror of your business. It shows you the naked truth about your business. It shows your unrealized growth potential.

Business Lens™ Diagnosis is the process of using Business Lens™ to perform a full analysis of your business, which identifies the areas that need more of your attention so you take your business to the next level.

Business Doctor is one of our growth programs, where we perform the Business Lens™ Diagnosis, and issue suggestions and recommendations for tactics and strategies to execute, so you grow your business immediately as well as long term.

Businesses don't grow unless people grow. You rock! By reading this book, you are enabling personal growth together with business growth!

Bonus:
Steady Growth - Systematize Your Business

Tactic #1

Follow a System

Focus your efforts exactly where they are required as your business grows

I have created the **Business Growth Focus Formula** (see below) because so often I see business owners focusing on the wrong things. You want to do what you like to do, or what you are best at and this is fine to a certain extent. But if you want to have a *highly successful business*, you need to approach it systematically, and change Focus according to which Stage your business is at. Focus doesn't mean you only work on a certain area of your business or that you do it all by yourself. It means you **concentrate your efforts on a particular area of your business at a particular time.** It also means that you learn more about that area. Of course, you can involve Experts and you can Delegate, as long as this area is where your mind is. Even if you outsource, you inevitably acquire more knowledge in that area.

Be disciplined and Focus on what you have to in order to reach your Objectives and fulfill your dreams

The idea is simple: your Focus, as the owner of the business, moves from 'Sales' to 'Sources and Resources' to 'Systems', as your company grows. This is the **best business growth strategy**. Focusing on one part of the business does not mean that you *only* deal with that part. It means, say, that you allocate half of your time to it, while the other half is split between anything else you would normally deal with. Above all, you, as the business owner, must focus on what needs your Focus, even if it is not necessarily what you *like* doing.

Let's talk about each area of a business:

Business Growth Focus Formula

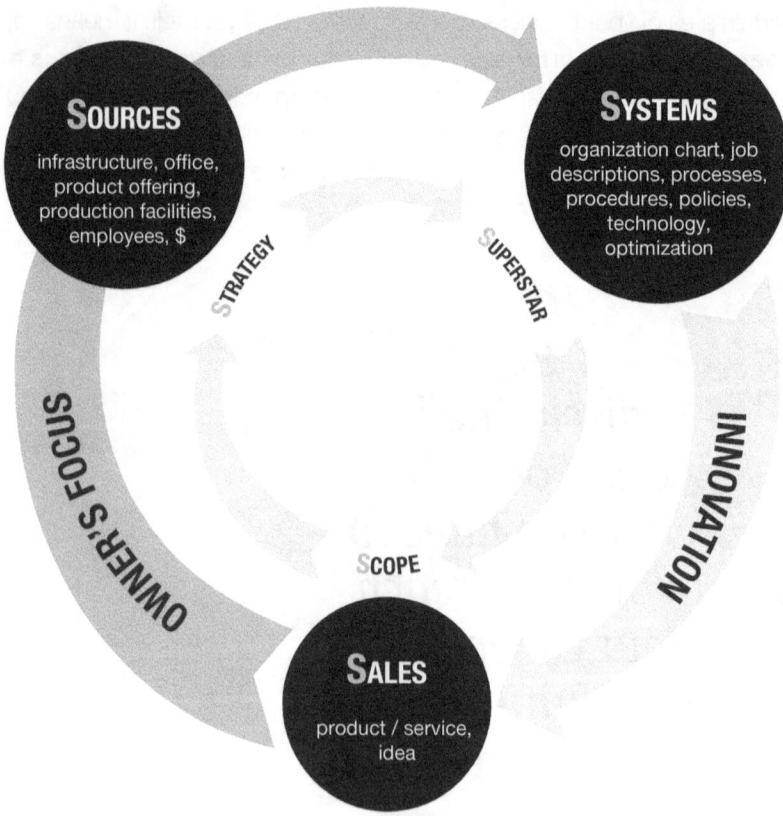

1 Focus on Sales

When you are at the beginning with your business, or when you launch a new product or open a new location. 'Sales' is split into two parts:

(i) selling your product or service;

(ii) selling your idea.

Selling your product or service is what you would generally understand as: giving your product / service to your customer in exchange for money (the price paid).

Selling your idea means getting people to buy into what you are doing. To share your dream, your vision and to get others excited about it. Selling your idea to current employees, potential employees, partners, suppliers, banks and any other person who is necessary to run the business smoothly, is as important as selling your product. You cannot create a business on your own. To achieve your Objectives, you need people around you. And those people don't join just because you think they should. It is tempting to believe they see and understand as you do, but they don't. You have to give them reasons to opt in, just as you give reasons to your customers to buy your product.

During this Stage, you have only a **Scope**. You know where you want to get to, but it is still flexible. You need the market reaction and partners' Feedback in order to ensure you have the right product, the right offering, both for your *customers* and for your business partners. The offering for the *customer* is a widely used concept: 'Buy this product for this price because it solves this problem in this way.' The offer for *business partners* sounds something like this: 'Bring customers to our business and you get x% from all the money they spend with us.' This is how you have to think of the Value proposition for your customers and your business partners. All parties have to win. And everything has to make sense and be clear from the outset.

2 Focus on Sources and Resources

Once your product or service sells by itself; in other words, when customers buy your product or service without you having to convince each of them individually. By 'Sources' I mean everything that enables you to deliver to your customer; that is, your overall infrastructure: production facility, office space, logistics, as well as your employees and money to buy raw materials and invest in further growth. No point selling if you can't deliver, right?

When you have gotten to this phase, **you have a Strategy in place.** Now that you know what and how you sell, and for how much, you can create Specific Objectives and a clear path to achieving them.

3 Focus on System

When you are confident that you have a product that sells and that you can deliver and satisfy your customer. By 'Systems', I mean organizational charts, job descriptions, processes, procedures, policies, IT system, and potentially CRM / ERP (software to help with planning and managing your Resources and your customers).

In this phase you **consolidate what you have**; you organize things internally and clean up your mess. By this Stage, you and your staff have tried various ways of producing and delivering Value and you now know who does what in your company, and how. It is therefore time to document everything that is happening in your company, to put order in place. This helps you and your current employees to better understand how things are being done in your company and to become more efficient. Having these Systems in place also makes for an easier and more efficient process when you bring new people into your organization. You have 'machinery' that works, effectively and efficiently.

What you care about now is **becoming a Superstar Company**. By 'Superstar', I mean being the best in your niche. If you think of your industry as a pyramid, there is only one company on top, a few on the second layer, then the third, and so on... until the bottom, where you find plenty of companies. Your Objective is to **get as close as possible to the top**. Why? Because if anything destructive happens in the economy or in your industry, or if anything happens that can adversely affect your business, you hardly feel it if you are on top. The financial crisis in 2008 resulted in many companies going bankrupt or being close to bankrupt – this is because they were at the bottom of the pyramid in their niche. If a tsunami comes, or the state does construction on the road in front of your shop or office, you need to be in such a strong position that your business does not suffer. This is being a Superstar Company.

After Systems are in place, you need to focus on **Innovation** if you want to take your company to the next level, in which case you go back to Sales in another growth cycle. Alternatively, you retire or sell your company (or you leave it as is and continue to manage 'in the business', which may eventually go downhill).

> *Shift Focus as your company develops and grows*

TAKE ACTION NOW!

Based on the Stage of your business development, decide which of the three areas discussed above requires your Focus. Write it down:

_____
_____
_____
_____
_____
_____

What are your biggest current Challenges? Write these here; then use the tactics in this book to find ways of overcoming these Challenges.

Challenge 1:
_____
_____

Challenge 2:
_____
_____

Challenge 3:
_____
_____

Challenge 4:
_____
_____

Challenge 5:
_____
_____

Sustain Your Business Long-Term

Tactic #72

Sustain Your Business Long-Term

Determine Your Product's 'Buying Criteria'

Satisfy a Need or solve a problem when you propose your product

Buying Criteria is a set of rules / algorithms / preferences that a prospect applies when making a purchasing decision; it is those factors that matter most to the buyer when choosing a product.

If you are a woman you will easily understand this: remember your list with characteristics of your dream man? What you look for when you search for Mr Right? (And sorry guys, I hate to break it to you: Mrs Right will have to have a lot more than big boobs and blonde hair!)

Understand what influences your customers to buy products like yours so you proactively influence their decision and tip the balance in your favor

Business Unlimited

Whenever someone buys something, they try to satisfy a Need or to solve a problem. Every person has different criteria they apply when deciding on the Solution to their problem. These criteria include all the information required by the customer to make their buying decision.

> The answers to these questions help the customer to make an informed decision:
>
> - What is it?
> - Why should I buy it?
> - What will I get?
> - What is the price?
> - Why do I even need it?
> - Why should I buy it from this seller?
> - What's the deal?

Each type of product or service will have different Buying Criteria. You need to really understand why people buy your product and what matters most to them. Examples of criteria could be: the look and feel, the credibility of the seller, the smell, the convenience, the price, the customer service, etc. Please note that each person could have different Buying Criteria for each product in different situations.

If it is hot outside and I want a cold drink or an ice cream, I will buy whichever I find first (so Buying Criteria is convenience). But if I want drinks or ice cream for a party I organize at home, my Buying Criteria is price, so I go to a large supermarket.

Usually people are not Experts in the field of whatever they are buying; i.e. in whatever you sell. **By knowing and fulfilling their Buying Criteria, you can teach every buyer how to be a better buyer of your type of product or service.**

If Häagen-Dazs tells me that their ice cream has half the calories of the lowest fat ice cream available in the street, I may wait and walk a bit further to get one of their ice creams; thanks to new information, my

Buying Criteria shifts from convenience to health (or the least unhealthy!).

The Milkshake story

Harvard Business School professor Clay Christensen regularly uses this story to show his MBA students how important it is determine the 'job' your product does... A fast food chain wanted to increase its Sales of milkshakes. They undertook major research to understand why people were buying milkshakes, and what the real Competitor / Substitute was for milkshakes. You might think a soft drink, a fresh juice or a banana. However, the research revealed that most milkshake Sales were being made in the morning, to customers who had an hour commute to work and wanted something to kill the time and have something to do with their hands. A banana is too quick to consume; same for a juice. A milkshake fulfills these criteria perfectly: due to its thick consistency, it takes longer to consume and involves putting the hands to use more times and over a longer period of time.

Once you understand your customers' Buying Criteria, you have two options:

(i) Match the criteria as closely as possible

(ii) Influence them (See Tactic #83 'Build Trust, Credibility and Respect' for more on this)

TAKE ACTION NOW!

Write down 5 Criteria that people use when buying the type of product / service you provide:

1. _____
   _____
   _____

2. _____
   _____
   _____

3. _____
   _____
   _____

4. _____
   _____
   _____

5. _____
   _____
   _____

Tactic #73

Create Your X-Factor

> *Apply fresh thinking to your business. What can we learn from Lady Gaga?*

Source/Autor: Victoria's Secret

An X-Factor is the secret ingredient that helps you achieve your Objectives faster. It is what you do better than your Competitors – better than anybody else. It is your competitive edge. It is also your aura of authenticity. Find your company's X-Factor and put it to work for you.

Creating your X-Factor is using your company's unique Skills and Resources to implement strategies that your Competitors cannot implement as effectively. And yes, you are part of those unique Resources! Your company's X-Factor could be anything from successfully revamping a product or service to developing a new process; from partnering with your Competitor to selling to customers you would never have dreamed of reaching; from reorganizing around customers instead of products to 'productizing' your service.

It can also be something that is unique about you, the founder of the company, which the business 'borrows' from you.

It is something that you need external help to spot. Most often, your customers will tell you, if you know what and how to ask. What's crucial is for you to 'see it' when you hear it (I didn't see it for 2 years, because I didn't know what to look for, and then it took me another year to nail it, once I knew what I needed - this is why I have now developed a process for this because most entrepreneurs don't have 3 years to wait! If you need support on this, contact me and I am happy to help.

Ideally, you want to really understand what is unique about you, your team, your product, your service... And combine everything you've identified, to make it stand out. Sometimes, this involves some creative thinking, sometimes you need outside expertise to package your X-Factor in something really desirable for your customers.

> *Every business can have such X-Factor.*
> *It is your job to identify it!*

Going back to college: I am sure you knew (or knew of) that girl who everyone wanted to go out with… she wasn't necessarily more attractive than any other girl, but she had this mysterious quality about her (which, for example, turned out to be her wicked sense of humor) and it meant guys were queuing to date her. Or the girl who, frankly, had terrible dress sense, but had guys wrapped around her little finger. Why? Her X-Factor was a kind of feminine fragility that men were attracted to, and her killer smile sealed the deal.

The X-Factor is your business's ability to add intangible Value – Value that goes beyond what anybody can measure with the usual tools. It is the ability to find a way to do more for your customers than anybody else does and to consistently maintain these high standards for fair prices.

There are likely to be plenty of businesses that do something similar to your business. However, no one does it exactly the way you do. This element is what differentiates you from the rest; it is your business's X-Factor. Your personality, your own X-Factor, is also clearly reflected in your business's X-Factor.

Know what your current X-Factor is, but also think about the future, and what your X-Factor should become. If something has never been done before, ask yourself why, and how you can use that to deliver more Value to your customers.

By finding your X-Factor, you find the advantage that puts you way ahead of Competitors in a key area like customer loyalty, pricing or employee retention.

Your X-Factor can leave your rivals miles behind you and unable to catch up. The discovery of your X-Factor also provides you with the clarity and momentum to produce the best long-term results and build a truly awesome business. Once you find it, keep it as quiet as possible so that your Competitors don't get it, but make sure you include it in your communication with your clients, so they come your way with no efforts on your side.

Failing to establish such a competitive edge puts your business in peril as it is then easy for others to sneak up from behind. The sooner you discover your X-Factor, the sooner doing business will become easier.

Learning from Lady Gaga

> *She can sing and play the piano, but it is how she 'shows up' that is totally unique to Lady Gaga. This is what has made her a Superstar. I am not suggesting pink hair or flesh suits; however, I am suggesting creating a style which is uniquely your own and represents who you are. Then, be consistent with it. This is how you 'show up' and how people will remember you. The entire customer experience you create is unique to you, and could be your X-Factor.*

Think of companies you buy from, and ask yourself why you choose them. For example, I love Starbucks – and I don't even drink coffee. My favorite drink is their caramel Frappuccino. I love the taste of this drink and have yet to find any drink that tastes as good. However, it is not just the Frappuccino I like about Starbucks. I love the coffee smell when I enter, the music, the overall atmosphere. It just makes me feel good when I am inside Starbucks. I have developed such a love for Starbucks that I miss it when I am in Brussels and will sometimes take a detour to pass by Gare Central to get my Frappuccino. In London, I always set up meetings in Starbucks. I know my way around London based on Starbucks. You get my point: they've got me. And they got me because of their carefully developed X-Factor. I can't tell you exactly what it is, but I know it is there.

TAKE ACTION NOW!

Write down 5 secret ingredients that will help you establish your business's X-Factor:

1. _____
   _____
   _____

2. _____
   _____
   _____

3. _____
   _____
   _____

4. _____
   _____
   _____

5. _____
   _____
   _____

Tactic #74

Use 'Core Story'

> *Tell Stories to communicate the advantages of your product while establishing a strong human connection with your customers*

In Tactic #11 'Tell Stories to Sell', we discussed the role Story can play in making your product personal and giving potential and existing customers a sense of ownership of the product. Developing a Story to tell your **prospects** will lead to a natural interest in buying your product. The Story should be able to create the Need for your product without you even mentioning it. The Story will also include any **Buying Criteria** you fulfill. Communicate your X-Factor (see previous tactic) in a way that is valuable to your audience.

The Core Story has to combine the power of data and research. In other words, include facts, statistics and numbers to prove your point. Facts alone, however, are not interesting. They have to be couched *within* a Story. Use more market data than product data to make your product or service appear more important. Market data is information generally valid about the market / population you are talking about, whereas product data is about a certain product or group of products. The more complex your product or service, the more data you need to use. This offers you the opportunity to appear as an Expert in your field.

> *As you include Buying Criteria in your Core Story, potential customers will naturally gravitate towards your product.*

Let's look at the Buying Pyramid below:

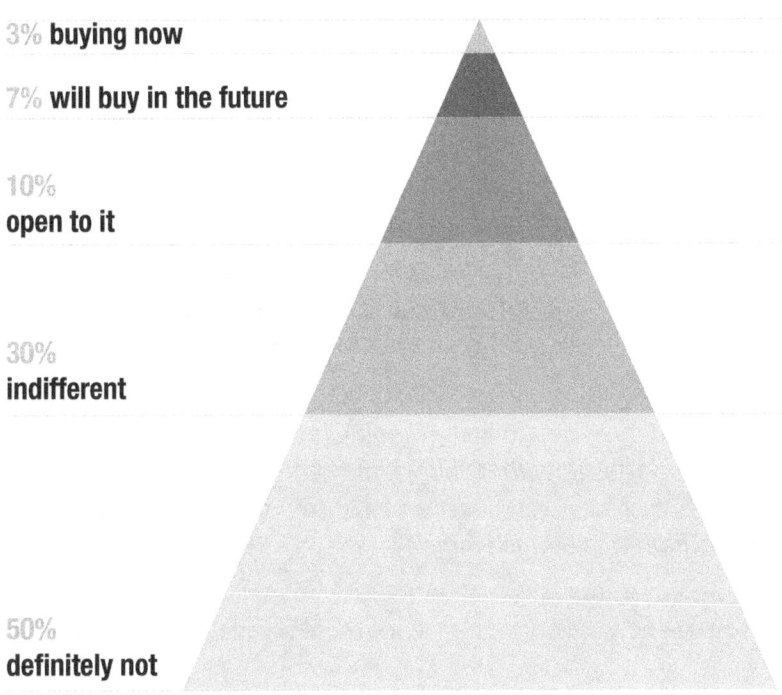

3% **buying now**

7% **will buy in the future**

10% **open to it**

30% **indifferent**

50% **definitely not**

Source: Adapted from The Ultimate Sales Machine *by Chet Holmes.*

Only 3% of people are ready to buy a certain product at any given moment. Another 7% are open to buying it in future, and the rest are not even interested. For people to become more open to the product you sell, they need a Story. The main point of this Story is thus to have them become more interested, and convert them into the group that wants to buy now; i.e. you want to increase that segment beyond 3%. This way, you increase the demand for your product, and you attract more customers to buy your product. As you include Buying Criteria in your Core Story, potential customers will naturally gravitate towards your product.

> *Help your potentials visualize how their life will improve after buying what you are promoting*

Here's how it's done!

Let's say you sell vitamins that help people live healthier and thus for longer. Only 3% of the population is actively looking to buy vitamins. Your Core Story could be along these lines: Vitamins help people be healthy and live longer. Research proves that 90% of people taking vitamins live on average five years longer than those who do not take vitamins (market data). Vitamin X (yours) has ingredient Y, which helps the body's cells regenerate twice as quickly as the ingredients in other vitamins (product data).

If you lived five years longer, imagine how much more you could do ... especially that you will be healthier. Thus in good shape to see places you never seen before, to play with your grandchildren and much more.

Did you see how a story can influence more people to buy vitamins?

TAKE ACTION NOW!

Write down 5 ideas you will incorporate in your Core Story. Take into account Need, Buying Criteria, X-Factor, Market data and Product data:

1. _____
_____
_____

2. _____
_____
_____

3. _____
_____
_____

4. _____
_____
_____

5. _____
_____
_____

Tactic #75

Train Everyone in Your Company to Say Something Valuable about Your Company

Strategic Communication is a fancy term for something quite simple: getting everyone (employees, customers, partners) used to saying something valuable about your company, products and services.

> *Everyone says something valuable about your company*

Encourage everybody in your company (you and your staff) to say something valuable about the company at every opportunity – no matter what the interaction is, no matter whom the interaction is with. You may want to have a meeting in which you explain to your staff how good it is for the company when they share what they like about working there. The staff could say what they are proud of, or mention aspects that resonate with them. If you get your staff excited about being in your company, this will come naturally to them.

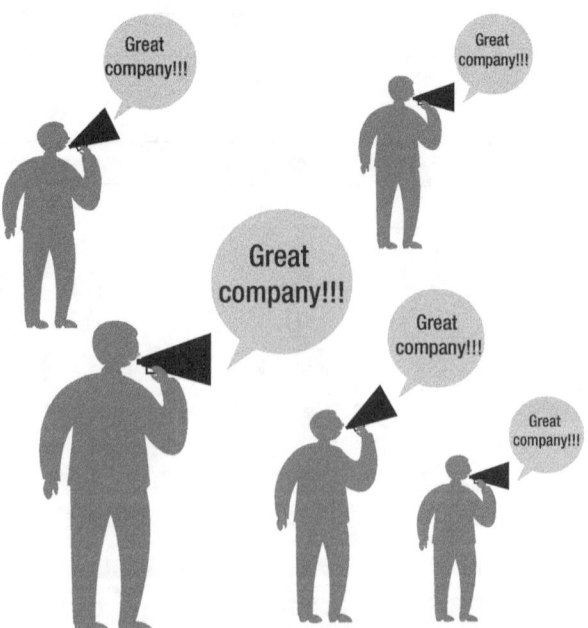

The more people that spread the word about your company, the better – even if no immediate business comes from it, or if the audience currently has no Need for your product. **If people are impressed with what you and the others say about the company, they will remember you, and they will contact you when they do need the product you offer.** Moreover, they too will spread the word if what you and your employees say resonates with them.

Think back to your college days again… you hear various guys talking about a blonde girl with blue eyes who always wears short skirts that show her beautiful legs. Apparently she is not only pretty, but also smart. You know she's in class 7B, so you take a detour via class 7B, hoping you will see her. What happened here? You got information about this girl from various sources and, curious, you did something out of your way to see her. Don't you think your potential customers might do the same if they constantly hear positive comments about your company?

This is what we like to see!

> *My colleague Valeriu bumped into a former colleague in the street. They went for a coffee to catch up and discussed life and work. Valeriu mentioned, with passion, how good we are at helping business owners grow their companies and shared various stories about Happy Customers. By the end of their coffee, his former colleague asked him if we could help his company grow, as he had been struggling to do so for years.*

> *Get your staff to spread information about the great elements of your business*

Anyone in the company can say something positive and of value about your company. The doorman might say: 'I love it there. Every morning, the two big bosses greet me with a smile and one brings me coffee every now and then!' This shows that the bosses care about their employees and the message transmitted by the doorman may have a positive impact when a potential future employee considers joining the company.

Here are some examples for inspiration:

- This is a great company. Not only do we offer top quality services to the client, but we, the employees, are also treated extremely well.

- We care for the environment; our company has a policy of saving energy.

- For every $1,000 we make, we donate $1 to the Save African Children Association, which feeds 3,000 children annually.

> By helping our clients, we are making the world a better place

> The doorman can be your promotional representative, spreading great messages about your company.

TAKE ACTION NOW!

Write down 5 positive elements that your team could share about your company. Once you have these ideas, make sure you Communicate with your team and Train them to convey these qualities to others.

1. _____
   _____
   _____

2. _____
   _____
   _____

3. _____
   _____
   _____

4. _____
   _____
   _____

5. _____
   _____
   _____

Tactic #76

Communicate Your Ultimate Strategic Position

> Hanging your mission statement on the wall doesn't do it anymore

Decide on your Ultimate Strategic Position (USP) – not to be confused with a Unique Selling Proposition – and make sure you and your staff communicate it all the time. The USP – the strategic positioning of your business – must always be top of mind. USP is what you want to be known for as a company, which is also part of the reason your customers purchase from you.

Your USP must be clear, and focused on what your customers get – not on what you offer; i.e. think of the benefits your customers receive first. For example, my USP for Tooliers® is: to become the premier platform where small business owners get the right affordable assistance to significantly grow their businesses and achieve their objectives faster, whilst investing the least time and money in growth'. This focuses on the customer. My USP is not 'we offer business growth services'.

Once you are clear on what you want to be known for, train your staff about your USP. Ensure they all communicate it, especially to your clients, prospects and business partners. Use any channel available: one-to-one discussions, PR, webinars, any marketing materials, videos, trade shows, to ensure your clients know what you want your company to be, and how you want to be perceived.

> Communicate the strategic positioning of your business, starting from your customer's side of the story

By highlighting the importance of your product and your company to your prospects (their benefits), you maximize the chances of selling. By having your customers and prospects perceive you as you want to be perceived, you attract more interest from the right

customers, and will be the preferred choice when prospects are ready to buy the type of product you sell.

Figuring out your USP may not be easy. In fact, if you want to do it right, you need to dig for more answers. The answers you need come both from your clients and yourself. You need a system to be able to figure out all your necessary answers. This is why I am doing a bootcamp on this subject. We spend two days together, going through my 7-step system to get to the Essence of Your Communication, so you can easily and clearly craft your marketing messages which attract clients in droves. Because this expresses your uniqueness as entrepreneur, which of course gives unicity to your business. This is a great start to eliminate your potential competitors, because this enables you to create your own space, where you dominate as the only potential supplier.

Check my 7 WHYs Bootcamp™ at **www.ozanagiusca.com/7-whys** and apply to be considered.

Once your USP is set and communicated, marketing it no longer becomes as big a deal. That's not to say you should forget all about marketing your product – just that your brand comes into its own and often experiences organic growth.

This is how it works!

> In college I used to organize huge parties. I would easily get 100 people to attend a party at my flat, in the mountains, at the seaside or even in a field in the middle of nowhere. People came to my parties because it was well known that the parties were fun and that beautiful people and the crème de la crème attended. Of course, at the time I didn't know anything about USP. I was just naturally throwing good parties, which people would talk about afterwards, and so word would spread. I got to the point where I could tell just a few people when and where the party was, and 100 people would show up. I didn't have to do the hard work of calling them (this was before the internet and mobile phones!).

TAKE ACTION NOW!

Write down 5 key points that make up your Ultimate Strategic Position:

1. _____
_____
_____

2. _____
_____
_____

3. _____
_____
_____

4. _____
_____
_____

5. _____
_____
_____

Tactic #77

Help Your Customers Achieve More Success

> *Don't get obsessed with selling: focus on discovering new and better ways for your products and services to improve your customer's life, and Sales will flourish naturally*

Gone are the days when you sold a product or service in your first meeting with the client and then said goodbye. Buyers are more educated and have more information available to them these days. They expect to get value for money, no matter what they buy.

Building Relationships with customers, continuing to communicate, and solving customers' problems are tactics we all know about. Your Competitors are already doing these. **You need something that goes beyond and gives true benefits to your customer: you need to help your customer achieve more success.** This really means caring about your customer and doing everything possible to make them more

successful. The more success you create for your customers, the more they will return to you or recommend you to others.

Currently, sales professionals tend to focus on pushing their product and achieving their numbers. They do not care much about finding Solutions that exactly meet the Needs of their customers. The Buyer-Seller Relationship is fundamentally broken. Let's face it, buyers don't trust sellers. They are tired of being sold to. The result for the sellers is often missed quotas and disloyal customers. This is unfortunate because, if you think about it, the buyer and the seller really do want the same thing: a Solution that meets the client's Needs.

There is a huge gap between how people want to buy and how businesses sell. Understand this gap, act accordingly and you will be in top 1% in your niche.

> *Fill the gap between how people buy and sell and you will be in top 1% in your niche*

You may think this tactic only applies to **B2B**, or businesses that sell training, personal development or career advice, but you would be wrong. It applies to every business. Yes, even if you sell ice cream or operate a parking lot, you can help your customer achieve more success.

This tactic can only be done once you really understand your customers. It is not just about understanding their challenges and needs, but also discovering what they want to BECOME. And position your product or service as the solution to helping them become what they want, have the business / life they want.

> *People love to buy but they hate to be sold to*

This is what we like to see!

When I was single in London, I used to go clubbing a lot. I particularly liked a new club called Elysium, on Regent Street. A month after it opened, I had a hot date. I really liked the guy and wanted to impress him. I arrived half an hour early for the dinner date and was walking past Elysium, when I saw the woman in charge of the guest list opening the doors. I walked up to her and told her I had a hot date and wanted to bring him to Elysium. Could she help me get in? She scanned me and then said, 'Sure, no problem. What's your name?' We introduced ourselves and I headed off to my date. She hadn't written my name down, so I wasn't sure she would remember me and keep her promise. After dinner, I suggested to my date that we hit a club. He agreed but said he doubted we would get in to any, as it is almost impossible to get into a good club in Central London on a Friday night. As we were approaching Elysium, my newfound ally saw me, said 'Hi Ozana' and asked the bouncer to let me and my date in. And you were wondering how a club could contribute to the success of its guests...

TAKE ACTION NOW!

Write down 5 ideas you will implement to help your customers be more successful and / or to improve their lives:

1. _____
   _____
   _____

2. _____
   _____
   _____

3. _____
   _____
   _____

4. _____
   _____
   _____

5. _____
   _____
   _____

Tactic #78

Sustain Your Business Long-Term

Create Clear Accountability within Your Company

> *Clear Accountability is a matter of well-defined ownership, sound delegation and good coordination within your team*

Accountability is the guiding principle that defines how we make commitments to one another; how we measure and report our progress; how we interact when things go wrong; and whether we take ownership to get things done. It is, in essence, the nerve center of every organization and affects every working relationship and every member of every team.

If this sounds complicated, here is a simple way to understand it. In college I came up with this brilliant idea to grind up chalk and sprinkle it on the professor's seat just before the physics class. No one in the class liked her and we all started imagining how funny it would be to see her skirt covered in chalk. Of course, no one wanted to follow through. As I had come up with the idea, I felt somehow Accountable, so I did it. I accomplished something. I was Accountable for (and yes, I was the one who was punished!).

You need to get your employees to be Accountable and do the things they need to do. In some companies one person performs more roles, and in other companies people work across various departments. Everyone wants things done quickly, which is impossible in many circumstances. People report to different managers for various tasks or responsibilities. So the more Accountable your staff are, the more structured the work will be and the more tasks will be accomplished.

If Accountability does not exist in your organization, then every effort toward performance improvement will be inefficient and ineffective. The ability to execute and deliver results is directly tied to the Accountability attitudes, practices and Systems that are in place in your company.

However, the real value and benefit of Accountability stems from the ability to influence events and outcomes before they happen. The customary view of Accountability fails to recognize that people can gain more from a proactive posture than from a reactive one.

> *Accountability will increase the responsiveness of your company to the Needs of your customers*

How to ensure Accountability (and how not to)

A real estate agency has to send weekly emails with new property alerts. Imagine the director of the agency says to his team: 'Please gather the offers we receive each week, and send these out to our database weekly.'

Now imagine he says this: 'Person A will collect all sale and rental offers and upload the information to our website within 24 hours of receipt of the offer. Person B is responsible for email marketing and will send the email highlighting new properties every Wednesday at 4 pm. This means person B will have to prepare the newsletter by noon on Wednesday and get my approval between 12 pm and 3.30 pm. If I am not available to review it, person C will do so. If person C is not available, person B will send the email without any third-party review.'

In the first scenario in the example above, 'the team' was responsible for sending emails, which left completing the task at their discretion. 'The team' means no one is actually being held Accountable. In the second scenario, however, responsibilities for sending the email alerts are clearly split between the team members and each member has clear and specific tasks and deadlines; i.e. they all know what they need to do and by when.

Some of the root causes for lack of Accountability include miscommunication from leaders and misunderstanding from employees. In other words, you say one thing and your employees understand another. This usually happens because you either do not have everything clear in your head, or are not able to express yourself so that people can understand you. The first step in creating Accountability is therefore to find out which it is, and make sure you communicate clearly with your staff, so they are able to be Accountable.

> *Accountability leads to things being done*

> *Lack of Accountability means job not done*

TAKE ACTION NOW!

Write down 5 ideas you will implement in the next 30 days to increase Accountability within your team:

1. _____
   _____
   _____

2. _____
   _____
   _____

3. _____
   _____
   _____

4. _____
   _____
   _____

5. _____
   _____
   _____

Tactic #79

Sustain Your Business Long-Term

Understand Your Business. Really!

> **Look beyond your direct Competition to understand what business you are really in**

How can I ask you, the owner of your business, to understand your business? Well, most business owners I meet don't understand. (Of course, you may be the exception.) Ask yourself: 'What business am I really in?' If you sell clothes, you may say you are in fashion. But if you are selling high-end clothes that are associated with a certain status, you may in fact be in the 'status' business (like Rolex).

When you consider your industry, think of why your customers buy from you. What Need do your customers satisfy with your product? What are the uses of your product? **Chunk Down** and **Chunk Up** to look at your business from different perspectives (see Tactic #36 'Be Efficient with Your Time' for more on Chunking). Let's assume you sell diesel cars. If you Chunk Down, you look at the type of car you offer: a five-seater five-door vehicle that uses diesel. However, if you Chunk Up, you are in the transportation business – you help people move from one point to another and you offer mobility. When you Chunk Down you look at your Competition strictly as other diesel cars. But if you Chunk Up, your Competition could easily be car rental companies, train companies, bus companies, the metro – anything that offers people mobility.

Once you know what business you are really in, it is time to understand what you are good and bad at.

Have you been pitching yourself in the wrong industry?

Be clear on why you have achieved your current level of success, and examine why you have not achieved more success.

See it in action!

Let's think of our client Jolyon who brings Leonidas, the famous Belgian chocolate, into Romania.

Are they in the chocolate business? You may say, 'Of course!' but I would argue they are in the gifts business. How many times have you bought Leonidas chocolates for yourself? How many times have you bought Leonidas to offer as gifts? I'm guessing more often for the latter.

When Jolyon realized he is in the gifts business, he started marketing his business difference and his sales went up!

While he was still selling Leonidas as chocolate, it was not easy for him to achieve good sales simply because people are not prepared to pay more for a chocolate than $1-$4, which is the usual price.

So, the same product (chocolate) with different packaging and positioning competes with different types of products or brands (luxury items or gifts). When you have it clear in your mind what your True Industry is, your entire marketing Strategy becomes focused on what you really are. You don't want to focus on other chocolate makers as your Competitors, and just have different packaging and position. Leonidas and Godiva use the superior quality of their chocolate and attractive packaging to compete in the luxury goods industry. Thus, they can command higher prices.

TAKE ACTION NOW!

Write down what type of business you are in:
_____

Write down 5 elements you could improve on now that you know your True Industry:

1. _____
_____
_____

2. _____
_____
_____

3. _____
_____
_____

4. _____
_____
_____

5. _____
_____
_____

If you are feeling unsure about your business or that is no longer serving you; if don't know your true industry; or if you simply feel you are losing interest in your business, check out our online masterclass "Design Your Business Model Based on Your Needs & Passions" *(www.ozanagiusca.com/your-business-model)*. It will help you identify what to change in your business so that you get what you want out of your business. Because when you combine your passion with your skills and offer something people want or need, you hit the jackpot!

Clarify Your Vision

> *Your challenge as a business owner should not be to keep your business on track but rather to make sure you are on the right track and switch to a better one if you are not*

Now that you really understand your business and which industry you are competing in, you need to decide where you want to go. Note that I didn't say where you are going – I said *where you want to go*. Do you want to be in this industry? Is this the right time to be in this industry? Are you passionate about this industry? Will it be thriving 10 years from now, or will it collapse and be replaced by something else? If the latter, what might that new future look like?

Traditionally, my company raised funds for small- and medium-sized companies. When Romania joined the EU in 2007, however, I started adding grants to my fundraising portfolio. With the banks disinterested in financing anything during the economic crisis, I ended up doing only EU funding of grants. There were fun times, and we managed to be among the top 10 consulting firms specialized in EU funding in Romania. However, a few years down the line I asked myself the questions above and realized I no longer wanted to be in this industry. In the EU funding industry, you are extremely busy during the submission process – the team does not sleep for days as deadlines approach – and this alternates with very quiet periods when there are no calls for proposals or projects open. We were also totally dependent on the Romanian authorities to evaluate the projects we submitted, and at times it could take three years to get your result! In that time the company might manage to complete the project for which it required funding, or it might abandon the project entirely due to market changes.

My Goal had been to help more clients get EU funding grants. After realizing this was not the right industry to be in, my Focus changed towards helping small businesses grow significantly... and build Smarter

Businesses which lead to the owners reach their objectives faster.

Think about it ...

> *List today's most successful companies with the fastest growth rates. Google, Apple, Facebook, Groupon, eBay, Amazon, PayPal, Booking.com... did you know these companies 15 years ago? Could you have imagined the types of services they offer 15 years ago? Do they influence the way we do business today?*

How will your industry be shaped by such companies? Internet and Technology are changing the business environment extremely quickly, and you need to be among the few winners, not the many losers.

You certainly don't want to have been in printed media or a travel agency in the traditional sense. Now rethink your industry, your position, and try to anticipate the future. If you struggle to see those opportunities, use the tools on our website *(www.tooliers.com)* to diagnose your business's Growth Potential and Challenges. You will immediately see what you are missing.

When you create your Vision, you need to ensure your business model is: sustainable, predictable, consistent. Clarify the Vision for yourself and for your team. Make sure you write down where you want to get and have a good plan on how to get there. Share this with your team. (See Tactic #51 'Share Short-Term and Medium-Term Goals with Everyone in the Company' for more tips on setting and communicating your Goals and Vision.)

> *Have a clear Vision and be flexible in your approach*

TAKE ACTION NOW!

Write down 5 ideas on your Vision for your business (and try to anticipate the future):

1. _____
   _____
   _____

2. _____
   _____
   _____

3. _____
   _____
   _____

4. _____
   _____
   _____

5. _____
   _____
   _____

Business rules are changing due to new technologies and as new companies emerge and people's habits change. Download your free 15 New Business Rules, so you can adapt your business to today's economy: *www.ozanagiusca.com/understand-the-new-rules/*.

Tactic #81

Create an Unstoppable Pre-emptive Anti-Competition Strategy

> *Use Pre-Emptive Strategies to be one step ahead of your Competitors*

A **Pre-Emptive Anti-competition Strategy** is a strategy designed to prevent any effective Marketing- and Sales-related actions from the Competition, and to encourage **prospects** to buy from you. It's a mouthful, I know, so let's go with an easy example: in your college years, you like a girl. The problem is that many others guys like that girl too; you have Competition. So you invite her to go to the prom with you. If she says yes, you have stopped your Competitors from being with her. There is only one prom! You win!

When you build Pre-Emptive strategies, you are unstoppable

In business, Pre-Emptive Strategies offer the best opportunity to gain advantage over your Competitors. **Pre-Emptive Strategies involve moving first to secure an advantageous position that rivals are foreclosed or discouraged from duplicating, or find impossible to do.** If you master this, you will attract buyers over all of your Competitors. And if you don't do it, your Competitors will be in the lead.

Think of the girl in the above example as the only Resource available to produce product X. If you could secure this Resource, you would be the only one able to produce product X. As a result you obtain a monopoly position for product X. This outcome may sound too good to be true… and it is. There are always more Resources available, and other types of products or Substitutes. Nonetheless, here are some examples of viable strategies you could consider to pre-empt your Competition:

- Secure exclusive or dominant access to the best distributors in an area.
- Secure the best geographic locations. If you sell flowers, you want to be in a busy intersection or metro station or railway station, where you have lots of traffic. If you want to significantly expand your business and pre-empt your Competitors, you need to open a flower shop in all such busy locations in your town.
- Tie up the best (or the most) raw material sources and / or the most reliable, high-quality suppliers via long-term contracts or backward vertical integration (when you produce your own raw materials). This move can relegate rivals to struggling for second-best supply positions.
- Last but not least, use **Educational Marketing** to 'educate' your market to use the 'right' **Buying Criteria**, which of course lead to your product being the natural choice, the only choice they consider.

Sustain Your Business Long-Term

Learn from the best!

You feel like a soda so you head to a corner shop, where Coca-Cola and a no-name cola are available. Which do you choose? Most people choose Coca-Cola; they might not even see the no-name cola. Why? Because Coca-Cola pre-empted their Competition by building a formidable brand.

TAKE ACTION NOW!

Write down 5 ideas to implement and create a Pre-Emptive Anti-Competition Strategy:

1. _____
   _____
   _____

2. _____
   _____
   _____

3. _____
   _____
   _____

4. _____
   _____
   _____

5. _____
   _____
   _____

Tactic #82

Sustain Your Business Long-Term

Inspire High Levels of Brand Loyalty

Think big: Branding is not for big businesses only

Before we talk about Brand Loyalty, let's get clear on what a **brand** is.

In December 2013, my partner and I went to the Rainmakers Summit, a Business Growth Workshop in Las Vegas, on a two-for-one ticket. He wasn't particularly keen to attend the summit (I was the one who wanted to go) and, while preparing for the trip, he said to me: 'If I don't like it, I will spend the day by the pool.' He was expecting temperatures of 30° C. We live in Europe and the only exposure he'd had to Las Vegas was through movies. All those wild and fun movies took place in a hot and sunny climate. Based on what he knew and had seen, he associated Las Vegas with great weather. This is branding! I'm not sure anyone set out to create such a brand for Las Vegas, but in my partner's mind, Vegas meant sun and loads of fun. Needless to say, it was below zero in Vegas during our visit, and when we went for a breath of fresh air at the Voodoo Club, on the roof of Rio All Suits Hotel, we felt as if we were on top of a mountain, ready to go skiing.

So what is a brand?

Your company's **brand** is what people say about your company when you are not in the room, when you can't influence them.

As for Brand Loyalty, it is the degree to which a consumer consistently purchases the same brand within a product class. When you go to the supermarket to purchase your washing liquid or toothbrush, you get the same brand each time, often without even thinking about it. Now it is time to think: why do you always purchase that brand? Because you know it delivers results. You trust this brand. You are so loyal that you don't even realize there are other brands out there that are equally good, or perhaps better!

You might argue, 'But I am not Colgate or Coca-Cola. Why would I create such a powerful brand?' True, but you can be the Colgate or the Coca-Cola for your target market, for your Best Customer. **You want your Best**

Customer to buy your product without questioning why, and without wondering what the alternatives are.

Get it right!

A client said to me: 'I sell garbage bags via supermarkets. I don't interact with the end-user.' He defined his client as the supermarket's merchandise buyer, not the customer at the till. 'Plus, everybody wants to buy the cheapest bag,' he continued.

It is true that everyone wants to buy the cheapest bag – provided they are all equal. But they are not. Some bags are thinner and they break while you take your garbage out if you overfill them. If you haven't experienced this it's because the seller of garbage bags in your area does a good job in educating you how to choose your bags, or you've learnt through trial and error and you get the right bag. That is the Best Value for money. When I explained to my client that he needs to stay close to his end-user and that he needed to educate him, and build Brand Loyalty, the penny dropped. His face lit up and he said: 'You are so right! Why did I never think about this? My bags are the best option, and they should be the most expensive, and people should buy them.'

> He then immediately brainstormed ways to create videos on YouTube showing his bags compared to others, to make in-store promotions, and to be close to his customers. Once customers understood the difference, they of course prefered his bags. And this is how they became loyal to his brand – which, when I initially spoke to him, did not even exist!
>
> Once he had achieved Brand Loyalty, his customers not only committed to his bags, they also told their friends his bags are the best choice. Word of mouth is the cheapest and most effective marketing tool. And yes, you can achieve it with Brand Loyalty.

Have a think: when you last bought a product you loved, **were you attracted to the brand**? Did you then buy other products from the same **brand**? Did you tell your friends how happy you were with that product? This is Brand Loyalty.

If you are used to buying Hugo Boss suits, when the crisis comes and you make less money, what do you do? Do you buy Zara suits or do you wait until you can afford another Boss suit? Did you know that these **brands** are the least affected by adverse economic situations? The reason? People get *emotionally* attached to their favorite **brands** and they stick to them no matter what.

Now start developing your own **brand**, no matter what you sell! If you are a very small business, your Personal Brand will be the **brand** of the business. So go build your Personal Brand. (See Tactic #59 'Brand Yourself' for some additional tips.)

Brand Loyalty equates to long-term, sustainable business success. You can count on loyal customers to keep buying your branded products and telling their friends about you. There is a value to that loyalty that correlates directly to brand equity, and therefore with the value of your whole company, which is directly linked to your future performance.

TAKE ACTION NOW!

Write down 5 ideas you will implement in the next 30 days to strengthen your or your company's brand and increase Brand Loyalty:

1. _____
_____
_____

2. _____
_____
_____

3. _____
_____
_____

4. _____
_____
_____

5. _____
_____
_____

Tactic #83

Sustain Your Business Long-Term

Build Trust, Credibility and Respect

> *Trust, Credibility and Respect are the key ingredients to acquiring both engaged employees and loyal customers*

Trust is the firm belief or confidence that a person or thing can be relied upon. If you buy a DVD player you expect it to work. You trust the seller / producer to give you a good, working DVD player. If you didn't trust the seller / producer, you would not buy the DVD player. No one wants to waste their time or money on a non-functioning product or service.

This is why you have to build Trust, Credibility and Respect for your **brand**, your business, your products and services – and for everything else you do. This pertains to your Relationships with the outside world (customers, business partners), and internally (your employees).

If your (potential) customers don't trust you, they will simply not buy from you. Your employees will take a similar position. How many people are willing to take (or stay in) a job in which they have to wonder at the end of the month: will I be getting my pay check or not?

'If I don't trust you, I will not view you as credible nor will I respect you. If I don't respect you, I will not see you as credible or trustworthy. If I don't find you credible, I will not trust or respect you.'

Dale Carnegie

The more trusted you are, the more benefits you will have. Your employees will have greater job satisfaction; they will be more committed and engaged in their work and in their relationship with your company. This leads to improved productivity, greater employee retention and, of course, better customer service, and satisfied and loyal customers.

They walk the talk!

> Stanford University consistently produces excellent results. Their graduates achieve on average the highest salary after graduation (any business school ranking will show you this); they find jobs in the shortest period of time; and they can more or less choose whom they work for. Stanford is consistently in the top ten universities worldwide. This is a university you trust to give you a good education and the tools to be successful. Stanford University has built Trust, Credibility and Respect by consistently delivering. So, if you wanted to study an MBA, which university would you want to attend if money or qualifications were not an issue?

Trust, Credibility and Respect are the three main ingredients to creating long-lasting customer engagement. You need all three to be successful because this is the only way to ethically influence the behavior of your *potentials* and keep them for the long term. This is about 'earning your influence'. **When you are reliable, deliver at all times and create Value for your customers, you earn the right – and privilege – to influence others.** Because they have seen consistent behaviors, actions and qualities and have come to value these, they let down their guard and allow themselves to be influenced by you.

> *Trust, credibility and respect are the ingredients to sell in 21st Century. They matter more than ever before.*

Good news is that you don't need to constantly meet your potential clients to earn their trust. You can do this via various online interactions. Your potential clients need to get to know you and understand you can really help them. And this can easily be done via various videos, or even blog posts or social media posts if you are not at the stage yet where you are comfortable with producing videos.

Our system, the Smart Business System™ consists of a combination of events and online interactions. I love events because they can quickly and easily build trust. And the sky is the limit, because once you build your system, you just put more money in advertising and get more clients. As simple as that!

> *Build your online and offline system so you easily earn your potentials' trust*

TAKE ACTION NOW!

Write down 5 ideas to build Trust, Credibility and Respect within and for your company:

1. _____
_____
_____

2. _____
_____
_____

3. _____
_____
_____

4. _____
_____
_____

5. _____
_____
_____

Tactic #84

Sustain Your Business Long-Term

Focus on What People Buy, Not on Your Profits or Sales

*Shift the Focus from the sale in sight
to Long-Term Success
by prioritizing your prospective customer's Needs*

There is a reason why you don't achieve the Sales numbers you want, and it is not due to weather or holidays or another bad decision taken by the government. It is because you don't give your customers what they want.

Have you ever been to Venice? Piazza San Marco is full of pigeons. Tourists feed them corn, bread and seeds (what the pigeons want) and in return the tourists get to sit among the pigeons and pose for great photos (what they want).

Apply this to your business: focus on what your customer wants (the pigeons obviously want to be fed!), and you will get the Sales and Profits you aim for. Develop Long-Term Sustainability for your business by focusing on your customer's Needs rather than on your Needs. **Putting the Needs of your customers ahead of your own is the solution for building a thriving business. An intense Focus on results can distract everyone from the Sales process.**

Customers don't care about your need to sell. They are concerned only with solving their problems. So focusing your Strategy to demonstrate how your Solution provides the greatest Value in solving their problems is key to your success.

> *Give your customers what they want and they will give you what you want*

This is what we like to see!

I am often criticized for not 'selling'. Well, I don't like selling, because I don't like to be sold to. When I meet prospects, I genuinely try to solve their problem and provide valuable information. I come up with Solutions and suggestions and I treat their business as if it were mine, providing the best advice I can. Last year, I was driving back to Bucharest from a meeting in Iasi, and I stopped in Roman to have dinner with the owner of a hotel there. She had fully refurbished the hotel to high international standards, but she had no customers. I gave her loads of suggestions during dinner. Instead of a relaxed dinner, it transformed into a work session. She was very keen, open and took plenty of notes. I liked it that she was so actively involved, so I offered to stay overnight and spend the following morning with her, working on her marketing plan.

The morning session was even more packed with actions and ideas. By noon, she had written about 15 pages in her notebook. And then she said: 'Ozana, you seem so knowledgeable about the subject... why don't you do it for me?' I landed a long-term contract for my consulting company, without me even thinking about selling it. Within one month we increased her Sales by 30% and we got a decent income out of this. I focused on her Need – to help her get customers – and my results (which I hadn't expected) came soon afterwards.

TAKE ACTION NOW!

Write down 5 Needs for which your product / offering is providing:

1. _____
_____
_____

2. _____
_____
_____

3. _____
_____
_____

4. _____
_____
_____

5. _____
_____
_____

Tactic #85

Associate with Trusted Organizations

As an upcoming brand, borrow popularity from Established Organizations

Association is a smart and fast way to gain authority and credibility for your own business. Being associated has many advantages, from having access to your partner's business customers (see Tactic #13 'Market to Your Partners' Customers') to borrowing influence from them. If your business is small at first, you can try to Affiliate with a better and well-known business to help solidify your business foundation. **If you are Affiliated with a well-known business, your own business will grow and increase in trust and influence.** That is why Affiliation is important early on in order to grow your business faster and more easily.

Have you ever broken down in the middle of the street and needed help to push your car to the side? You created an 'Association' with the aim of moving your car out of the way. What alternatives did you have? To call AAA and get them to move the car – but that would have taken longer. And what if you didn't have AAA membership? The Association you created was free, quick and easy and, most importantly, it solved your problem instantly.

What if you could apply the same technique to your business? Here are some examples of Associations you could create, and why:

- **Affiliation to an international organization.** As a hotel owner, you could be Affiliated to the Best Western chain. As a gas station owner you could be Affiliated to Shell. This type of Association adds credibility to your business, which means more Sales in the long term.
- **Associate your unknown product with a well-established company.** As a new smoothies drinks company, have your product available in all the cafés belonging to a reputable chain. If this is too long a shot, start by having your product sold in a popular local café. This will push the Sales of your product, because that café's

customers trust it, and thus trust is 'transferred' to any product in the café.

- **Associate with More Successful People.** This is called Branding via Association. So you 'borrow' from the brand of the other person for your own advantage.
- **Join a Mastermind group.** Find the right group for you, one where you can equally contribute and get good advice. Mastermind groups or communities are meant to help each other do better. The idea of masterminds is that one person can benefit from many other minds giving advice and suggestions to overcome Challenges. You will have access to thought leaders and mentors who can provide you with key business intelligence, helping you manage your business more effectively to achieve better top and bottom line results. For example, I have created the *Ozana's Inner Circle™* to support small business owners solve their problems, build and grow further their Smarter Businesses.
- **If these sound too complicated, start by joining a Chamber of Commerce or a Trade Association in your field.** This will open doors to the Association's members, so you can explore common interests and potential business opportunities. Your voice will be heart and you will feel more comfortable until you develop your own brand.

For more ideas on different types of Partnerships, see Tactic #25 'Develop Partnerships'.

This is what we like to see!

As an EU funding consulting firm, we could not voice our problems about the EU funding system in Romania, which was more dysfunctional than functional. Two smart consultants formed an Association, which we joined, along with 50 other EU funding consulting firms. All of a sudden, our voice was being heard by the government officials, and we could contribute to the improvement of the EU funding system.

Developing Long-Term Relationships with trusted and reputable partners is essential for Long-Term Sustainability of your business. No one person or business can do it alone. According to *American Business Magazine*, 'approximately 85% of all business failures occur in firms that are not members of their trade association'.

I am not that keen on Trade Associations because we have built our Smart Business System™ which enables us to scale our business without depending on anyone, without needing any help because we figured how to use social media advertising to generate leads. So sales are coming our way right now on autopilot. However, I felt more comfortable being part of associations prior to having built our system.

We can make a difference together!

Because business is complex these days, and because my mission is to change the world by empowering 1,000,000 entrepreneurs to achieve their objectives smarter and faster, I've created the **Ozana's Inner Circle™**. This is an organization where determined entrepreneurs are working together with me on every important aspect of their businesses so we all achieve our objectives faster.

If you want to eliminate struggle and really enjoy your business growth journey, I would happily consider your application to become a member in the **Ozana's Inner Circle™**.

Find out more here: ***www.ozanagiusca.com/inner-circle***

SMART Business System™

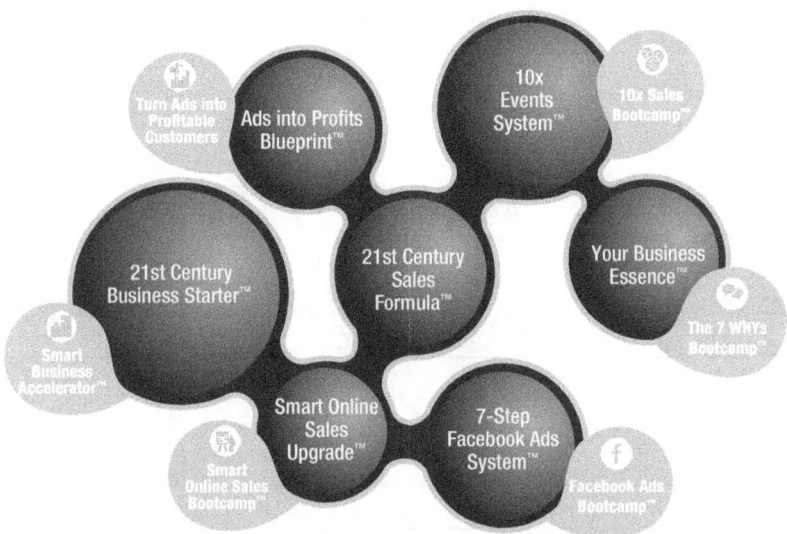

When you join the Inner Circle, you will have access to our entire system which we leveraged to gain clients on all continents. We transfer the knowledge to you via a series of events, where we work on specific areas of your business that need a tweak to be fit for 21st century business environment, so you achieve smarter profits faster.

TAKE ACTION NOW!

Write down a potential Partnership or Association you will pursue within:

1. International organizations:
_____
_____

2. Mastermind groups:
_____
_____

3. Trade associations:
_____
_____

Tactic #86

Be 'Online Social'

> *To be or not to be on Facebook?*
> *Your future customers are already there*
> *and they expect you to join the party*

These days you cannot afford not to be on social media. You have to go where your clients are. Like it or not, they are on Facebook!

Make social media part of your Marketing Strategy; combine it with other marketing tactics. See social media as another communication channel, but one that works two ways: from you to your customers, and from your customers to you.

Make sure you use it to communicate with your clients only once or twice a day, quickly and efficiently. Once you have posted, responded to comments

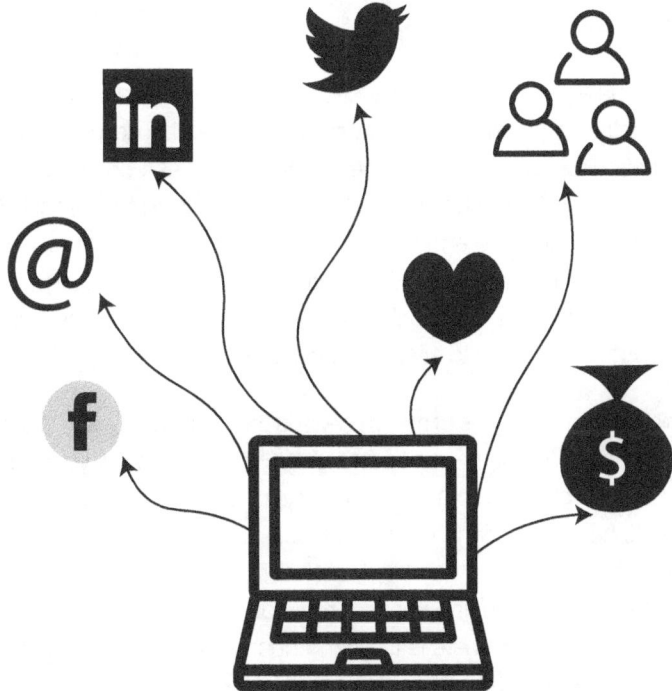

and finished what's required of you, get out of there. Don't get into the trap of wasting valuable time on Facebook! You have work to do!

Turn Facebook on. Turn Facebook off

If you're a skeptic, you won't expect much out of social media, at least not in the short term. But your clients expect you to be there – and if you don't regularly talk to them in social media forums, your Competitors will.

A great approach to social media is to think of it as a way to engage more with your customers. **Use games, special deals, and promotions to keep them close.**

You might say, 'No, I sell to serious people. They're not on Facebook.' Go search their names and let's talk afterwards. Unless you sell to my father's generation (70+), your clients *are* on social media. And most importantly we are building trust with our potential clients by our activity on Facebook, so more entrepreneurs come our way because something they had seen on Facebook.

I confess I was against social media for a long time. I considered it a waste of time. I don't want to know when my neighbor walks his dog, or when my former primary school friend has a new date. But I was convinced by the younger staff in the firm to use it, and I am already seeing the benefits. We share our blog posts, tips and tricks and other info with our audience on social media. And most importantly we are building trust with our potential clients by our activity on Facebook, so more entrepreneurs come our way because something they had seen on Facebook.

One of the great advantages of social media is the ability to engage with your customers. Communicating with customers who 'like' or follow your page is easy and direct. You are also able to involve your customers more by asking them questions and getting direct Feedback on your product or service. Managing this Relationship can be intensive if you are a big **brand** (most companies hire Social Media Experts for this purpose), but a key benefit of engaging with your customers is to strengthen Brand Loyalty – customers feel they 'know' you and your **brand** becomes personal.

Social media also offers some valuable analysis tools for business owners. You can see how many people have viewed your posts, for example, and determine which are more effective in creating Sales and why.

> **Use any Social Media platform to generate hot leads into your Sales Funnel**

There's more to it than you think!

Summertime Publishing, who helped with the editing of this book, also runs expatbookshop.com, an online portal for books by expats about expat life. Traffic to the website was ticking along slowly until the publishing house created a Facebook page for Expat Bookshop. Suddenly the views per post increased dramatically. One reason is that the Network had increased significantly, as all Summertime Publishing staff had announced the Facebook page to their Networks, who had announced it to their Networks, and so on. As more people 'like' or follow the page, it gains greater publicity and reach. The Facebook page has driven more traffic to the website and those who enjoy the content and find it relevant often subscribe to the blog.

Though I resisted it at first, we are currently getting most of our clients from Facebook advertising. Ok, we did make some rookie mistakes, but when you crack it, Social Media advertising is a gold mine. Go to **www.ozanagiusca.com/facebook-ads-templates-blueprint** and grab your Facebook Ads Templates, so you post proper ads – ads that people actually click – and generate business for you!

Social Media advertising is something I have recently discovered myself and since I mastered it, I am getting hot leads on autopilot. Go to **www.ozanagiusca.com/sales-funnel-blueprint** and grab your Effective Sales Funnel Blueprint, which can help you generate business online even if you suck at marketing.

TAKE ACTION NOW!

Write down 5 actions you will undertake in the next 30 days to increase your social media reach:

1. _____
   _____
   _____

2. _____
   _____
   _____

3. _____
   _____
   _____

4. _____
   _____
   _____

5. _____
   _____
   _____

> Social Media works wonders when you send traffic into a sales funnel, rather than to a sales page or your website. Read exactly how to do it here: **www.ozanagiusca.com/sales-funnel-blueprint**

Smart Business System™

In my experience, which includes being responsible for increasing the profits of 100 companies over the past three years – in some cases doubling and even tripling profits – I've noticed that most people running a small business or working alone, face 7 main challenges to increasing sales.

Many believe their lack of further success is due to legislation, taxation, red tape, banks not lending or the government not helping small businesses, but the truth is there are 7 challenges that are within your control to overcome, which makes all the difference.

It is important to understand these challenges, to identify which ones you are facing and then to use the very best system to overcome your specific challenges.

Because I also faced these challenges, specifically when I was struggling to sell with Tooliers *(www.tooliers.com)*, I have developed the **Smarter Business System™**, which is our battle-tested solution for achieving objectives faster.

My team and I have been using this system on a daily basis. Initially we kept it for ourselves and for a select group of clients. Now, we share it freely with fellow entrepreneurs, experts and driven professionals who want more.

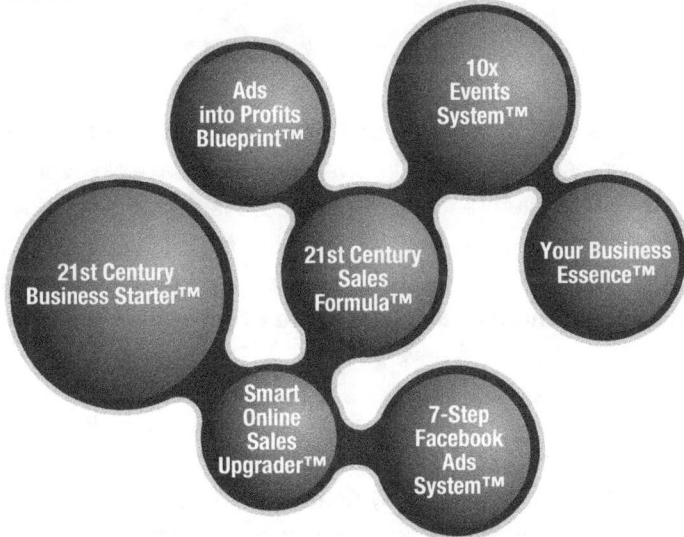

It is my pleasure to invite you to my online or live Master Classes in which I detail the system and its components.

Join me wherever it is convenient for you. Select from the events listed at **www.ozanagiusca.com/my-events** whatever best suits you and your needs. Some events are free and some require an investment.

Below I share more about the 7 challenges that block the growth of most businesses as well as the sub-system I have developed to overcome each challenge.

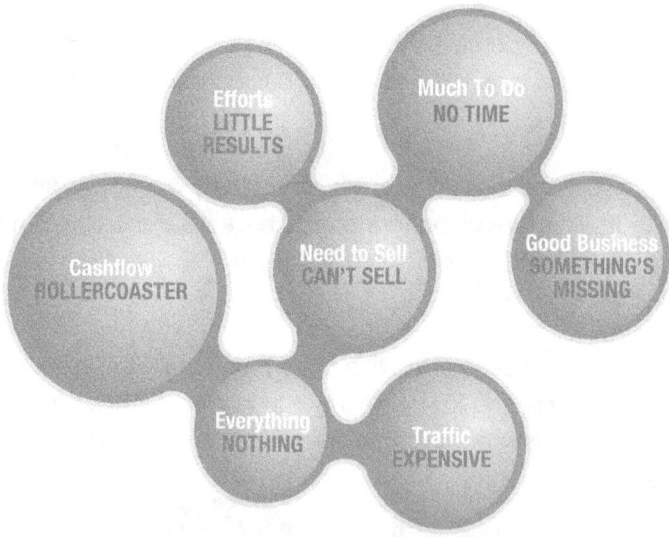

Challenge #1

Small business owners **want to sell more and have a stable, solid income**. Increasing the sales involves having a saleable product or service, a sales system and a way to feed this system with potential leads. Because there are various potential issues that need to be addressed before a business really takes off and grows exponentially, the **cash flow of most entrepreneurs is often like a rollercoaster** (sometimes up, more often down).

Too many meetings end up being a waste of time. Networking may be okay for social reasons, but few people buy from those they meet at events. A potential client suddenly goes cold... and whatever we do, it seems that people are simply no longer interested in buying.

Today, **people don't buy the way they used to**.

Due to the technology developments and the internet, the way people buy has changed. Which means that if you want to sell more, you also need to change your approach.

You need to adapt your business to the current reality. This is having the 21st Century Business Approach, the 21st Century Business Marketing Methods, and the 21st Century Business Essentials (this is not about the essentials in your business, which I am sure you have, but about the essentials that your business needs to give to you, its owner), because business as usual, as in the past, is no longer an option.

The key words here are Customer's Journey, a term that many experts talk about, but which is not understood and leveraged as it should be. This is about you **building a number of pre-programmed interactions with your potential clients, so you take them from "I don't know you" to buying from you and even recommending you to others**.

In most cases, such a 'journey' doesn't happen naturally. You need to engineer it, so your potential clients take the right steps (depending on where they are in relation to wanting your type of product or service) towards you and only you.

In order to build the road for such a journey, you need the 21st Century Business MAP.

21st Century Business MAP™

Smart Business System™

Deploying this system is the way to not only stay in business long term, but to thrive and generate increasing cash flow.

We are talking about combining online with offline activities, about talking to the potential client more but mainly in an automated or semi-automated manner, so you really leverage what you have and know so you achieve smarter profits faster.

I discuss this new approach and how to position your company, product or service and how to build your Customers' Journeys during the Smart Business Accelerator™ *(www.ozanagiusca.com/kim-en)*, strategic workshop over two days.

If you want to be in full control of your business; if you are fed up with trying various approaches which waste your money and time only to bring stress and frustration; and if you are committed now to investing to transform and scale your business, to maximize your profits and increase your impact so you achieve YOUR objectives, then I'm here to support you!

I invite you to join me for my next workshop where we will plan your Smarter Business *(www.ozanagiusca.com/kim-en)*.

Challenge #2

Before they started working with us, our clients were doing various activities, trying to sell to as many people as possible, but only getting a few clients.

I often see entrepreneurs busily developing a new product, serving existing clients, trying to source extra help, doing the admin tasks and even taking the trash out. They are constantly busy, feeling overwhelmed by how much they have to do… but what progress do they actually make?

For these entrepreneurs, I have developed the **Smart Online Sales Upgrader™**, to enable you to get more and better clients fast. Because generating business online can be done on auto or semi-auto pilot and when the system is deployed correctly, you have more time to do what you really love.

See in the illustration below how you can deploy this method to build your own system, to generate business online and have a constant and predictable cash flow.

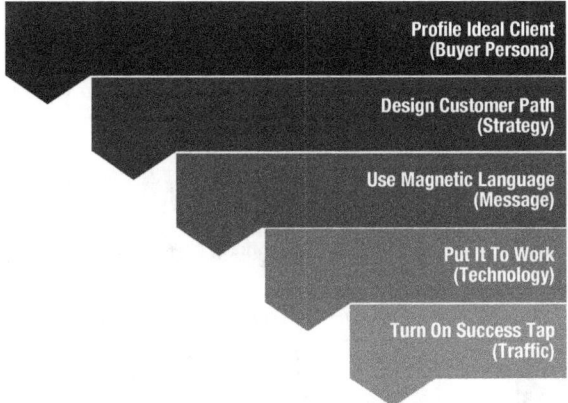

Under our guidance, participants in our Smart Online Sales Bootcamp™ *(www.ozanagiusca.com/sos-bootcamp-en)* achieve in two days what they have struggled to do on their own for years!

This method works because it has been tested on more than 400 entrepreneurs in most industries, ranging from professional services (consultants, coaches, experts) to manufacturing and retail.

The secret here is CLARITY. And to get clarity you need to go through a series of questions and, of course, answer them systematically, on paper.

Challenge #3

The majority of small businesses want more traffic in their store (online or offline) or visiting their website. Traffic is expensive, though, and they can't afford to waste resources on promotional activities that don't lead to sales.

We've figured that Facebook is the best platform right now to get traffic. It works for all businesses, but only when deployed correctly. If you are wondering if Facebook Ads are for you (i.e. investing in promotion on Facebook), join my next online Master Class *(www.ozanagiusca.com/facebook-ads-why-en)* on this subject.

Smart Business System™

We have developed the 7-Step Smart Business Facebook Ads System which we'll present during this Master Class. Simply go to **www.ozanagiusca.com/facebook-ads-system-en**, register, attend, take notes and implement.

We tested and tested… invested $100,000+ in our own campaigns and helped 300+ clients run profitable ads campaigns.

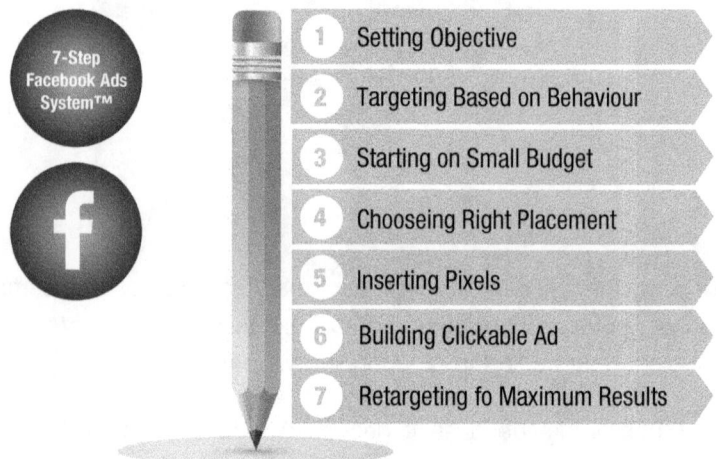

7-Step Facebook Ads System™

1. Setting Objective
2. Targeting Based on Behaviour
3. Starting on Small Budget
4. Chooseing Right Placement
5. Inserting Pixels
6. Building Clickable Ad
7. Retargeting fo Maximum Results

Challenge #4

Many people running their own show, be it a one-man venture or an established business, **need to sell but don't know how**. The truth is that selling is a skill you can learn. What's interesting is that most of our clients don't want to even consider taking sales courses. Because, just as they don't like others trying to sell to them, they know their potential clients don't want to hear from another pushy sales person. Besides, we set up our businesses based on our passion, because we want to help others and change the world, and we don't want to sound like second-hand car salesmen!

Many of my clients find themselves in a catch 22: they know their product or service is excellent but clients only realize and appreciate the value once they've experienced the product. Unable to clearly explain this amazing value to their potential clients, they have to constantly decrease their price just to make a sale.

The solution is the **21st Century Sales Formula™**, which is about helping your potential clients in advance so you show them, before asking for the sale, that you are the right person to help them.

The secret is to do it in such a way that you **create interest for your product or service so you don't even have to "sell" for a sale to happen**.

Imagine your best clients coming to you and begging you to sell to them!

Join my next Master Class on How to Accelerate Your Sales *(www.ozanagiusca.com/accelerate-sales)* to discover how easy this is. And yes, this is exactly what I do – I create interest and earn the trust of potential clients (like you) by offering real help in my Master Classes without any sales talk.

The more value you create in your marketplace, the more offers you can make. And of course, the more offers you make, the more sales you can achieve.

21st Century Sales Formula™

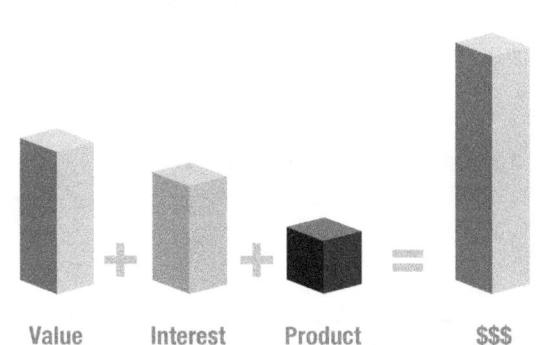

Value   Interest   Product $$$

Challenge #5

Most people in business have invested money, time and a lot of efforts in promotion, but the results are far from satisfying. This is because many tactics have been used in isolation without a strategy to back them up.

If you feel you have this challenge, then I highly encourage you to discover my Ads into Profit Blueprint™, where you can get answers to your burning questions about advertising, and more importantly, where you can ask more questions to help you get the RIGHT answers. Yes, it is only when you ask yourself the right questions that you can get helpful answers, so you can really get a good return on their promo budget.

Access Ads into Profits Master Class *(www.ozanagiusca.com/turn-ads-into-profitable-customers)* to get the right answers to the right questions.

Most entrepreneurs gain business in the traditional way. What you'll understand is how to expand beyond what you do well and break through the current sales figure, by adding other products, services, actions.

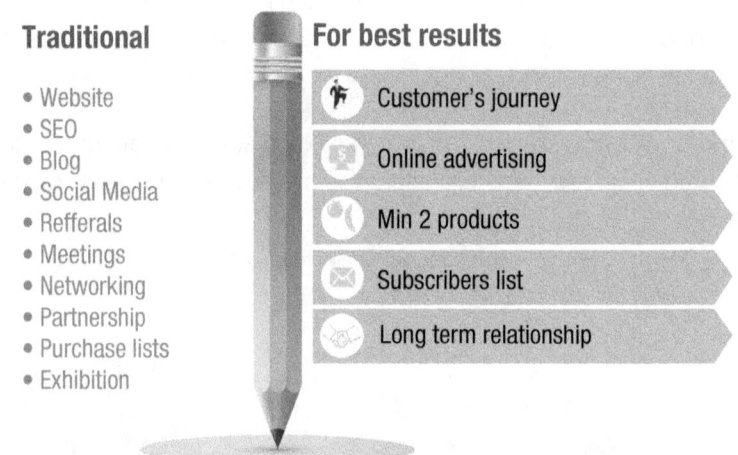

Traditional

- Website
- SEO
- Blog
- Social Media
- Refferals
- Meetings
- Networking
- Partnership
- Purchase lists
- Exhibition

For best results

- Customer's journey
- Online advertising
- Min 2 products
- Subscribers list
- Long term relationship

Challenge #6

Most people in business have a lot to do and not enough time to do it! They wish the working day had 48 hours so they could hold more meetings with potential clients and show their product to more people; to ultimately increase their sales and profits.

Well, there is a way for you to have 50 to 500 sales conversations in an hour or so. If you're asking yourself how this is possible, the **10x Events System**™ *(www.ozanagiusca.com/10x-sales-bootcamp-en)* is for you.

Instead of giving away valuable information about your product or service during a sales conversation, share it in an educational or fun context, when your potential clients WANT to hear you talk about your offering.

The benefit of selling at events is that it is the most efficient way to sell, while getting your potential clients to love you for the experience and information you provide.

What do I mean by 'events'? It could be a workshop, a webinar, a series of online videos, a sampling / tasting or networking event, even a fashion show.

As you become closer to being an important player in your niche, you need to consider selling from the stage/ via events. This is not just for experts and trainers. Our clients who have introduced events in their marketing and selling activities include fashion, car repair, consultants, kids development, agricultural equipment, even doctors.

Of course, we are not talking about just any event! There is a way to hold events of the highest quality, which I share with you in the **10x Events System™** *(www.ozanagiusca.com/10x-sales-bootcamp-en)*.

Challenge #7

Whether an established business or a newcomer, we all want to make more money. For some, money is a means to living the desired lifestyle, and for others it's a means to show they've achieved a lot and gained the appreciation and respect they deserve.

The challenges are that due to daily activities, and fires that need to be put out, entrepreneurs forget about their destination and most often behave as if lost in a dark forest.

In addition, in a world with so many people trying to sell so much it is difficult to grab your clients' attention. In a world where it is hard to get the right employees, and where communication is so important... it is not easy to 'construct' the right messages that attract the right people. You need to formulate your messages, with a view to ensuring that they are short and to the point, but most importantly, that they get to the heart of your potential clients. Such communication depends on the clarity you have about yourself and your business, and the connection between the two.

Unless you have a set of key messages that you and your team consistently use, you are just another seller, talking in generic terms like most people. This means you are forced to keep your price to a minimum, rather than getting paid for the real value you provide.

In other words, you need to carefully draft your key messages to use as your introduction, as a conversation opener or even on stage when you speak in front of more people. In order to get it right, you need to go to the essence of your business.

This is YOUR job!

No external consultants can come up with your key messages because they have to represent you. And the good news is that when you work on identifying such messages, you'll reconnect with your business and fall in love with it all over again.

The outcome is the right foundation for your communication, and you'll really become unstoppable and truly fulfilled when you answer the 7 WHY-based questions shown in the illustration below.

Big companies spent tens of thousands of dollars to identify their key messages. We've created a process to help you distill your key messages without spending an arm and a leg.

Would you like to overcome any of these challenges?

Then I invite you to join my **Smart Business Accelerator™** *(www.ozanagiusca.com/kim-en)* to discover how to build your Smarter Business, your business anchored in the current reality, and adapted to your current needs, aligned to your heart, so you feel in control and get to your destination faster.

Let's spend two days together, and you will

- Evaluate your growth opportunities to unleash the full potential of your business

- Eliminate time wasters, so you really focus on what is most important for you

Leave this workshop with clarity, ways to upgrade your business and a plan of action so you achieve your objectives faster.

Bonus: Love Letter

More value to you

I write about giving more Value than anticipated to your clients, about amazing your customers, about giving something for free. Here, it is my freebie to wow you.

Following, you will find the easieast way to come up with your marketing strategy. I give you the tool so you define your marketing strategy in 30 minutes. The tool is in the form of a letter you write to yourself as if it was written by your Best Customer. I call it 'Love Letter' because it shows the love your customers have to your company. It looks like a testimonial, but it is much more than that. Fill in the blanks. The point of this letter is to help you really understand your business, and what matters for your business's success. It looks like a testimonial, but it is way more than that. Once this letter sounds right, you know the recipe for your business's success. You have more clarity about your own business. You just need to execute correctly (You can do that by applying the 101 tactics in this book).

Below you will find a template for your Love Letter, as well as the letter I wrote for Tooliers®. This helps me 'name' my Persona, the benefits of my product (both logical and emotional), the impact my product has on customers' lives, how to find our customers, what to use to find customers, what I want my customers journey to be, how to ask them to provide recommendations, and more.

This template is your Strategy in a nutshell! And yes, you can use this to get inspiration for what you want your (real) client testimonials to look like.

I challenge you to fill in the blanks for your business. If you want the original, so you don't have to type up the template, visit **www.ozanagiusca.com/love-letter/** and grab your copy for free.

Love Letter Template

Dear **[Company Name]**,

My name is **[Persona's name]** and I must tell you I love your **[product type]** and I feel compelled to tell you my story.

I am a **[business type / life or lifestyle role]** who **[problem / passion statement]**. Thing is, that **[impact of pain / passion to life]**.

But **[Product Name]** changed my life.

Whenever I **[do specific things with product]** it works exactly as promised. Not only do I **[specific benefits]** but it makes me feel **[strong emotional reaction]**.

I find I use the product in that way every **[time period: hour / day / week, etc.]**

It's as if you looked me in the eye and said, '**[Persona's name]**, I promise you **[value promise]**'.

What I didn't expect, and share with other **[why shares with]** by **[mean of 'sharing']** is that you made me feel **[emotion impact]**.

Your product has forever **[how life changed]**.

I first heard of your product while **[activity / place related to title or life role]**. I decided to learn if it was really meant for me, so **[how to get more info]** where you said **[key message promise]**, which spoke directly to me. To tell you the truth, at first I was skeptical. But then, when you provided **[activity to induce trust]** I knew you were the right company.

[Influencer] endorsing the product was also key.

Still, I felt **[primary concern / objection]**.

Finally, when **[final action]** I was ready to **[sign up / buy / try]**.

I couldn't wait to get going, so as soon as I could, I **[first product setup / interaction]** to get started, and very quickly tried the **[feature to realize promise]** which made me feel hopeful that I had made the right decision.

Love Letter Example

Dear Tooliers®,

My name is Elisabeth. I must tell you that I love your Marketing Lens™ Diagnosis and Growth Program and I feel compelled to tell you my story.

I am an accounting firm owner who needs more clients. Thing is, I'm not earning enough. But Marketing Lens™ has changed my life.

Whenever I think of investing in marketing activities, I use the Marketing Lens™ and it works exactly as promised. Not only do I discover free ways to attract clients, but it also makes me feel like I really master marketing as a whole. I find myself working on one action to grow my business every other day, for only 15 minutes per day. I started this just one month ago and I already see 10% more enquiries from potential clients.

It's as if you looked me in the eye and said, 'Elisabeth I promise that you will discover ways of getting more customers by yourself without spending a cent.'

What I didn't expect, and I share this with other accounting firm owners in our regular ACCA meetings, is that you made me feel like a great businessperson, not just an accountant. I truly *feel* I own my business now; I am not just a simple accountant who has a job in my own company.

Marketing Lens™ Diagnosis and Growth Program has forever changed how I market our accounting services.

I first heard of your product while browsing The American Institute of CPAs online. I decided to learn if it was really meant for me and I went to www.tooliers.com. You said that I would get answers to questions I had never asked myself and this really resonated with me. To tell you the truth, at first I was skeptical about getting actions tailored to my business and given automatically to me by a computer! No one knows my industry better than me. But then, when you provided the Marketing Lens™ Diagnostic Report I knew you were the right company. Your assessment of why I was not attracting the customers I wanted was spot on. You also showed me what I need to focus on attracting the customers I deserve.

Entrepreneur.com's endorsement of Marketing Lens™ Diagnosis and Growth Program was also key to my decision to check you out. They are a trusted resource with information for every business owner.

Still, even at this stage I felt marketing was too complicated for me. Besides, I truly love performing accounting services, *not* marketing my business. Finally, after having followed the Action Plan on Social Media, I was ready to buy the Marketing Lens™ Growth Program. I understand now that things are not as complicated as they seemed, and that even I can attract and engage online with potential clients for my firm!

I couldn't wait to get going, so as soon as I could, I performed the Marketing Lens™ Diagnosis. I quickly started with the first action on Sales Funnel Tactic, which made me feel comfortable that I'd made the right decision. I see how, by the end of the Growth Program, I will have become a marketing guru for my business; customers will come to us, as bees are attracted to a honeypot. And you know what? I now see myself as *managing an accounting practice*, and no longer as doing accounting services. The latter is the job of my employees!

> **Want to grow your business and don't know how and where to start?**

> **Or do you have a business challenge you want an expert opinion on?**

I love bringing new ideas to the table and contributing to the growth of any kind of business, from e-commerce sites to professional services providers; from retail to entertainment. Every industry has its own particularities, but all have one thing in common: **apply best business practices and your business will succeed.** It's exactly this subject that I've mastered, and I can help any business implement best practices, regardless of size, industry or geography.

So contact me via my website and I'll respond within 24 hours.

www.ozanagiusca.com

If you just want to stay in touch, connect with me on:

- www.facebook.com/giusca.ozana
- plus.google.com/+OzanaGiusca
- www.linkedin.com/in/ozanagiusca
- www.twitter.com/OzanaGiusca
- www.youtube.com/user/ozana197

Glossary of Terms

These definitions are crafted to be as simple as possible, and are explained in the context of this book.

AAA rating - refers to the evaluation of credit worthiness; i.e how trustworthy a company is to do business with. The highest rating is AAA, descending to C (low) and D (even worse).

Action Plan or Fast Track implementation Plan - a step-by-step guide to work on and improve various areas of the business (strategy, sales, marketing, etc.) and sub-areas (educational marketing, writing blogs, building a website, email marketing etc.).

Affiliate Marketing - this is an agreement whereby a business rewards someone (affiliate person or company) for each visitor / customer brought by the affiliate's own marketing efforts, or for each purchase generated by the affiliate, within a time frame.

Attractive Premium - an item included in a pack, together with less interesting items, and sold as a bundle. It's a good way of moving slow-selling products.

Automate / Automating / Automation - using software rather than employees to undertake automatically some processes within the company.

Business-to-business (B2B) - a business that sells to other businesses. Compare with Business-to-Consumer (B2C), which is when the company sells to consumers / individuals.

Better Offer - a product (service) or a bundle of products (services), designed to offer more value (than usual) for the same dollar spent.

Brand - the name, design, symbol, colors or any other feature that identifies one company or product. For example, Coca-Cola is one brand, Fanta is another; they both belong to The Coca-Cola Company.

Branding via Association - linking the brand of one business with a better known brand, so the lesser known brand 'borrows' from the popularity of the other.

Business Doctor - business growth solution consisting of (i) diagnosing a business (see Business Lens®), (ii) designing a customized action plan to optimize and grow the company and (iii) implementing that plan.

Business Lens® - company assessment toolkit to show business owners the naked truth about their company. It identifies unexploited growth potential. It covers everything that matters for the growth of the business (analyzes in detail 15 business dimensions, including Strategy, Innovation, Leadership, Superstar Organization, Marketing, Sales, Human Resources, Motivation, Support Systems, Follow-Up and Organizational Culture) a Tooliers® service.

Business Lens® Diagnostic - the process of answering multiple choice questions and getting a business evaluation report that shows what the business does well and what it needs to focus on a Tooliers® service.

Buying Criteria - the requirements and rules that one buyer uses to buy a product, such as quality, price, availability, reliability, durability, comfort, habit, safety, freshness, coolness, taste, production methods, etc.

Chunking - grouping together information into ideally sized pieces, so they can be used effectively to produce the outcome one wants without stress or shutdown.

Chunk Down - dealing with smaller parts of information / activities in order to understand or do them effectively. Especially useful when the information / activities are new or complex.

Chunk Up - dealing with larger parts of information / activities in order to understand / accomplish more at once. Especially useful when one faces known information or deals with routine activities

Complementary Product (Service) - product (service) whose use is interrelated with the use of another product (service); e.g. cartridges and printers are complementary products.

Cross Selling - one business selling its product (service) to another business's customers, and vice versa.

Distribution Channel - the path through which products travel from vendors to consumers; e.g. coffee travels from farmer to exporter, to importer, to distributor, and to the retailer who sells to the end user.

Educational Marketing - sharing valuable information with potential customers, for their benefit and to build trust.

Gift with Purchase - providing another product (service) when someone buys a certain product (service); e.g. a sample cream when you buy a perfume.

Host-Parasite Relationship - adding one's product to be sold passively together with another product that is marketed and sold by the other business (the 'parasite' company doesn't do anything to make sales happen). E.g. producer of a dress adds belt from another manufacturer, and promotes and sells the dress with the belt.

Inducement(s) - an incentive to make the offering more appealing to the customer, and the sale sweeter.

Joined Offers - offering one's product together with another product; both parties promote the combined offer.

Joint Venture (JV) - business agreement for a set period, in which each party undertakes some efforts, for the benefit of all parties.

Lead - term used for a potential customer in the first stage of a sales process; i.e. the business made the initial contact with that prospect, be it (directly or indirectly) via the business's website, or via a phone call or meeting.

Lead Nurturing Email - email designed to build relationships and trust with prospective customers in a consistent and relevant manner.

Limited Edition - the manufacturing of a product in a limited quantity, to make it a more interesting purchase for the buyer.

Limited Time Offer - an offer that has a specific deadline, to give potential buyers a clear reason to act without delay.

Limited Stock Offer - a limited number of items made available, to give potential buyers a clear reason to act without delay.

Locking Sales In - securing long-term sales; e.g. signing a long-term contract or ensuring customer comes back for repeat purchase.

Offer Email - an email to promote a product, to ask for a purchase.

Potentials or Prospects - potential customers.

Pre-emptive Anti-competition Strategy - a strategy employed by one business to lead potentials to only consider its offering, thus blocking its competitors even before they are considered by the buyer as potential sellers.

Risk Reversal - marketing strategy based on removing the risks of the buyer to help them make the purchase decision; e.g. 30-day money back guarantee.

ROI (Return on Investment) - a performance measure calculated as the benefit produced by an investment divided by the cost of that investment (expressed as %); commonly used to evaluate the efficiency of an investment or to compare different real or potential investments.

Glossary of Terms

ROTI (Return on Time Invested) - the return on the time invested into an activity or project (valued in dollar amount per hour).

Sales Funnel - a metaphoric description of the sales process from initial contact to final sale. It is called a 'funnel', because there are many leads (cold potentials), and as one gets closer to the sale, the number decreases.

- Attract
- Engage
- Nurture
- Sell
- Deliver

Soft Skills - a cluster of personality traits, social abilities, communication, language, and personal habits that characterize relationships of one person with others.

Tooliers® - online platform with business growth tools designed to help small and mid-sized business owners to take their companies to the next level. Founded by Ozana Gusca.

Ultimate Strategic Position (USP) (not to be confused with Unique Selling Proposition) – the final perception that a company wants to have in the eyes of the customer.

Unique Value Proposition (UVP) - a few words used by one business to tell prospective customers why they should buy their product or use their service; it tells how this business adds more value or better solves a problem than competing businesses (similar to Unique Selling Proposition).

Value Papers - promotional materials (such as flyers, leaflets, brochures, catalogues) that give, besides the usual information / advertising content, monetary value to the holder towards the purchase of the product / service being promoted (such as % discount, $ reduction, gift); the goal is to incentivize a sale.

> *'Any ending is a new beginning.'*
> Ozana Giusca

Make the most of the knowledge you have received or gotten from this book and take your business to the next level.

In this series

www.ozanagiusca.com/BusinessUnlimited

www.ingramcontent.com/pod-product-compliance
Lightning Source LLC
Chambersburg PA
CBHW070301230526

45470CB00002B/667